Book

Lover's

Devotional

Book

Lover's

Devotional

WHAT WE LEARN ABOUT LIFE

FROM SIXTY

GREAT WORKS OF LITERATURE

BARBOUR
PUBLISHING

Cover design: Faceout Studio, www.faceoutstudio.com

Published by Barbour Publishing, Inc., P.O. Box 719, Uhrichsville, Ohio 44683
www.barbourbooks.com

Our mission is to publish and distribute inspirational products offering exceptional value and biblical encouragement to the masses.

Member of the
Evangelical Christian
Publishers Association

Printed in the United States of America.

Contents

Introduction

If you like books, you'll love this collection of sixty readings that draw engaging, contemporary spiritual points from literature.

From George Orwell's *1984* to *Winnie the Pooh* by A. A. Milne, the books included in this devotional run the gamut from literary classics to lighthearted romps. You'll find several centuries' worth of great reading profiled.

Each entry features details on the book itself, then describes a moment of truth to be found in the story. Though various writers take very different approaches to the Christian faith, they often pose insightful questions—questions the Bible is ready and willing to tackle.

After each book profile, "For Further Thought" questions encourage you to think critically about the story and how its questions relate to your life.

We hope *The Book Lover's Devotional* will remind you of some great moments in your favorite stories. . . introduce you to unfamiliar books you might want to read. . .and, more importantly, get you thinking about the deeper meanings of both literature and life.

1984

Author
GEORGE ORWELL
(BORN ERIC ARTHUR BLAIR),
1903–1950

First published
1949

Original publisher
SECKER AND WARBURG, LONDON

Notes
- ONE OF *TIME MAGAZINE*'S
  "100 BEST MODERN NOVELS"
- FILM VERSION STARRING JOHN HURT, 1984,
  RICHARD BURTON'S LAST FILM

THE MINISTRY OF LOVE

*A*side from George Orwell's beautiful writing style and wonderful imagination, there is *nothing* inspirational in the novel *Nineteen Eighty-Four*. It is a near-relentless nightmare where peace has come to mean war and love has come to mean hate, where the past is perpetually re-written and the future is a jackboot grinding a human face forever.

This miserable, wretched world is controlled by "the Party" and the invisible-but-omnipresent Big Brother. Winston Smith, a party functionary, becomes convinced that he and others like him are "the dead" and decides to rebel. He has an illicit affair with Julia, a coworker, and approaches O'Brien, whom he thinks is sympathetic to the rebellion, about a rebel group intent on deposing Big Brother.

He convinces himself that freedom is the ability to say, "Two plus two equals four."

It's a short-lived rebellion. O'Brien, the party's torturer, takes Winston Smith to the Ministry of Love, where he brainwashes him into believing that two plus two equals five. Despite this, Winston still manages to keep something of himself. He still hasn't betrayed his love for Julia.

O'Brien takes his prisoner to Room 101, the place where everyone confronts his worst fear. For Winston Smith, this takes the form of a two-part cage: One part fits around his head and the other holds starving rats. As O'Brien opens the dividing gate, the last decent part of Winston Smith disappears. He betrays Julia, knowing she will be tortured in his place. He puts her between himself and his nightmare.

Reintegrated into "normal" life, Winston Smith cries tears of gratitude as he realizes how much he loves Big Brother—though at that moment he would love a bullet in the head every bit as much.

Orwell's vision is a world without God. Human love has become worthless, and there is no hope. His world is indistinguishable from hell. Big Brother is indistinguishable from Satan.

We, on the other hand, *do* have God—and that's where we should find our inspiration. And there's more! Room 101, in whatever form it may take, can never steal our souls. We don't have to sacrifice love. God has already put someone between us and hell: His own Son.

Christ lifts us above Winston Smith and "the dead" to an everlasting future where peace means peace and love means more than we could ever imagine.

*Who gave himself for our sins to rescue us from the present
evil age, according to the will of our God and Father.*

GALATIANS 1:4 NIV

For Further Thought

1. In what ways can you see or feel the world
    trying to get you to conform to its own way
    of thinking and behavior?

2. In your own words, how would you
    describe the love of God and what it
    means to you?

I've read this book ❑

My Star Review ☆ ☆ ☆ ☆ ☆

ALL QUIET ON THE WESTERN FRONT

Author
ERICH MARIA REMARQUE,
1898–1970

First published
SERIALIZED IN *VOSSISCHE ZEITUNG* IN 1928,
PUBLISHED 1929

Publishers
PROPYLÄEN VERLAG, GERMANY
LITTLE, BROWN & CO., ENGLAND

Notes
- BANNED AND PUBLICLY BURNED BY THE NAZIS
- THE 1930 FILM WON ACADEMY AWARDS FOR
  BEST PICTURE AND BEST DIRECTOR

A Night in the Trenches

All Quiet on the Western Front is a poignant story by Erich Maria Remarque, a German veteran of World War I. The story transcends cultural and social barriers, showing the undeniable horrors of war.

The hero in the story is a young German boy named Paul, who goes off to fight for his country during "the Great War." One powerful scene in the midst of battle haunts many readers because it is so brilliantly written and because it speaks so clearly to the issue of loving our enemies. In this scene, Paul is separated from his company in the heat of battle. He hides out in a bomb crater, exhausted and terrified. . .and completely alone. The unthinkable happens when a young French soldier jumps into the trenches with him. Paul's knee-jerk reaction is to attack.

What happens next is shocking to most readers. Because of the impending danger outside the crater, Paul is forced to spend the night with his wounded enemy. This young man dies a slow and painful death, and Paul, know-ing he is to blame, is overwhelmed with emotion as he watches. After all, his "enemy" is not much older than Paul himself.

Can you picture it? Two men in the trenches together . . .one alive and one dead. One German, one French. One battling his emotions, the other battling no more. As the night progresses, Paul grows more remorseful. He realizes that the young man he has killed is not his enemy at all. He's just a fellow victim of war. Paul goes through the deceased man's things, learning his name and discovering he has a wife and child. When morning comes, Paul is reunited with his fellow soldiers, but he is haunted by his treatment of his so-called enemy.

Picture yourself in that bomb crater, spending the night with someone you see as an enemy. Who do you envision? Think about that one person you struggle with the most. Who is in the trenches with you right now? Have you hardened your heart, or are you speaking words of life over the situation?

Show love to the very person who has hurt you the most. Do good to the one who hates you. Pray for the one who spitefully uses you. Forgive. Bless. Love. It's truly the only way to face the morning light with a peaceful heart.

But I say unto you, Love your enemies, bless them that curse you, do good to them that hate you, and pray for them which despitefully use you, and persecute you.

MATTHEW 5:44 KJV

For Further Thought

1. How do you think you would respond to someone you see as an "enemy" if you were to allow yourself—just for a minute—to try to see things through his or her eyes?

2. What should be your response to your enemies, to those who treat you wrongly or dislike you for no particular reason?

I've read this book ❑

My Star Review ☆ ☆ ☆ ☆ ☆

ANNE OF GREEN GABLES

Author
LUCY MAUD MONTGOMERY,
1874–1942

First published
1908

Original publisher
L.C. PAGE & CO., BOSTON

Notes
- MORE THAN 50 MILLION COPIES
  SOLD SINCE PUBLICATION
- THE FIRST OF MANY FILM AND TV
  ADAPTATIONS WAS MADE IN 1919

A FATHER TO THE FATHERLESS

*F*ew stories in literature encapsulate the message of our Father God's heart for His children like Lucy Maud Montgomery's classic tale *Anne of Green Gables*. Anne Shirley, the story's young heroine, represents each one of us. She comes to Green Gables a fatherless child who hasn't quite found her place in the world. In a sense, she is a lost soul. Others have taken her in, but they haven't really cared for her—at least not in the way she needs.

There is a somewhat ironic scene near the beginning of the story in which Matthew Cuthbert (the owner of Green Gables, a farm in the town of Avonlea, on Prince Edward Island) goes to the train station to pick up an orphan child that he believes to be a boy. He and his sister Marilla have decided to take the boy, because Matthew is growing old and needs help with the chores at Green Gables. Imagine his surprise when he finds Anne—a darling little chatterbox with red hair—waiting there. He takes her back home to meet Marilla. Unfortunately,

Marilla—who is rather stoic in personality—doesn't take to the child. Anne is everything Marilla is not: quirky and fun, and often into mischief.

Anne feels set apart from the other children in Avonlea, not just because of her "plight," but also because of her physical appearance. She despises her red hair, even going so far as to dye it. Unfortunately, the dye turns her hair a lovely shade of green! In one of the most poignant scenes of the book, Marilla helps Anne cut her hair, promising one day all of this will be behind her. Surely she refers to more than just the green hair!

In spite of her challenges, Anne maintains a hopeful view of life. She's convinced that "God's in his heaven, all's right with the world." In fact, her story ends with that very positive message. All of this is made possible because two people extend a hand to her, offering love and hope in her time of need.

Our journey is much like Anne's. We come to God broken, without a home, lost, and unsure of where we fit in. He fathers us, caring for our deepest needs and offering a safe place to run. Then, as we are healed and made whole, He teaches us to do the same for others—to extend a hand to those in need.

As others receive your love, may they, like Anne, come to understand that "God's in His heaven, all's right with the world."

Defend the poor and fatherless:
do justice to the afflicted and needy.

PSALM 82:3 KJV

For Further Thought

1. In what ways do you see yourself as "broken and lost" before God? What did He do to make you healed and whole when you came to Him?

2. What specific actions can you take today to "defend the poor and fatherless" who are around you?

I've read this book ❑

My Star Review ☆ ☆ ☆ ☆ ☆

AROUND THE WORLD IN 80 DAYS

Author
JULES VERNE, 1828–1905

First published
SERIALIZED IN *MAGASIN* AND PUBLISHED IN 1873

Original publisher
PIERRE-JULES HETZEL & CIE, PARIS

Notes
- UNESCO LISTS VERNE AS ONE OF THE FIVE MOST-TRANSLATED AUTHORS EVER
- THE 1956 FILM WON FIVE ACADEMY AWARDS FROM EIGHT NOMINATIONS

THE JOURNEY HOME

*J*ules Verne's *Around the World in 80 Days* is a romp. From a standing start, Verne's hero, Phileas Fogg, and his manservant, Passepartout, embark on the ultimate adventure: to travel around the world in eighty days—just to prove it can be done. If they don't succeed, Fogg stands to lose half his fortune.

As the story begins, Passepartout is looking for a quiet life and Phileas Fogg is the ultimate stay-at-home. So far, so good. Then, as it usually does, life intervenes. The whole world intervenes, in fact.

Fogg determines to set out on his epic journey the same evening he made the bet. He seems like a man who has everything, but he has no friends or family to say good-bye to and no commitments to delay him. He thinks of himself as a man who needs nothing and no one. The journey will change all that.

Fogg and Passepartout make good time at first. Their schedule is planned to perfection. It only falls apart when they stop to rescue an Indian girl, Aouda, from a sacrificial fire. It's against the clock all the way from there.

Arriving back in London, Fogg is convinced he has lost the bet. He must surely be penniless, but he doesn't care because Aouda has agreed to marry him. Then Passepartout realizes that by traveling from west to east they have actually gained a day. They win the bet!

But the costs of the journey equal the winnings. Fogg isn't broke, but he's no better off—at least materially. He still doesn't care.

Just like Passepartout and Phileas Fogg, you and I might prefer to stay at home, enjoying the quiet life, going to church and saying all the right things. We're only here a short time, though, and, as our heroes find out, there are people out there needing saving.

Phileas Fogg's riches come from a source that is never explained and that his associates don't understand. After his adventure, he still has them and he has love as well.

A loving God provides our riches, which will stay with us always. At the end of our journey (which can be every bit as wonderful in its own way as Phileas Fogg's) we will return home no richer or poorer than when we arrived. . .unless we managed to love or be loved along the way, because that's what makes the journey worthwhile.

"What good is it for a man to gain the whole world,
yet forfeit his soul?"

MARK 8:36 NIV

For Further Thought

1. Other than the material ones, what kinds
    of riches has God blessed you with both
    today and in the past?

2. In what specific ways can you use the
    riches God has blessed you with to enrich
    the lives of those around you?

I've read this book ❏

My Star Review ☆ ☆ ☆ ☆ ☆

AT THE BACK OF THE NORTH WIND

Author
GEORGE MACDONALD, 1824–1905

First published
SERIALIZED IN *GOOD WORDS FOR THE YOUNG*, 1868
PUBLISHED IN BOOK FORM, 1871

Original publisher
STRAHAN & CO., LONDON

Notes
- C. S. LEWIS AND J. R. R. TOLKIEN WERE ADMIRERS OF MACDONALD'S WRITING
- MACDONALD CLAIMED NOT TO WRITE FOR CHILDREN BUT FOR "THE CHILDLIKE"

THE GOOD SIDE OF SUFFERING

*I*n his fantasy work *At the Back of the North Wind*, Victorian storyteller George MacDonald introduces Little Diamond, a boy named for his cabbie father's favorite horse, Big Diamond. This tale of young Diamond's adventures with North Wind, a glorious woman with pale skin and long dark hair, tackles the truths of God's goodness even in the face of the world's seemingly endless evil and suffering.

One night as Little Diamond sleeps in his loft above Big Diamond's stall, North Wind blows a knothole from the wall, awakens him, and invites him to ride on her back. Before they begin, she warns him that she doesn't always look beautiful, that sometimes she swoops like a huge bat or howls like a vicious wolf. But as long as he holds tight to her hand, it will never change in his.

On one journey, North Wind takes care of Diamond with one hand while sinking a ship with the other. When he questions how she can be good to him while being cruel to others, North Wind says that since "there can't be two mes," she must be either good or evil. Diamond knows she's good and learns that sometimes what looks cruel isn't really. North Wind only does the tasks set for her by "Another," and each person receives whatever treatment is best for him or her.

Diamond suffers horribly on his journey to the back of the North Wind. The cold nearly kills him, but he returns after a time, always longing for that beautiful land at her back. When North Wind tells him that people call her Evil Chance and Ruin and another name "which they think the most dreadful of all"—Death—Diamond learns that he's never been to North Wind's back at all, that he's only seen its shadow. But at book's end, because it's the best possible good for him, he dies and enters the true land at her back.

Sometimes we as Christians have trouble understanding the purpose of pain in this world. We can't see the good in the suffering around us. But as North Wind explains to Diamond, sometimes good things must look ugly because they are "making ugly things beautiful." In His wisdom, God often uses the hard things in our lives to fulfill His plans for us, plans to give us a future and a hope. Although our sufferings may seem hideous, God uses them to conform us to His image and prepare us for our own journey to the land at North Wind's back.

"For I know the plans that I have for you," declares the
LORD, "plans for welfare and not for calamity
to give you a future and a hope."

JEREMIAH 29:11 NASB

For Further Thought

1. How do you respond when an honest
   skeptic asks how a loving God could allow
   so much suffering to go on in the world?

2. What specific good have you seen come
   out of your own suffering or the suffering
   of those close to you?

I've read this book ❑

My Star Review ☆ ☆ ☆ ☆ ☆

AULD LICHT IDYLLS

Author
J. M. BARRIE, 1860–1937

First published
SERIALIZED IN *ST JAMES'S GAZETTE*, 1888
PUBLISHED IN BOOK FORM, 1888

Original Publisher
HODDER & STOUGHTON, LONDON

Notes
- A COMPILATION OF VIGNETTES DEPICTING VILLAGE LIFE IN SCOTLAND
- THE *AULD LICHTS* OR "OLD LIGHTS" WERE A TRADITIONALIST SECTOR OF THE SCOTTISH CHURCH

SNECKIE

J. M. Barrie is best known for writing *Peter Pan*, but in his *Auld Licht Idylls* there's a little scene worth thinking about.

The narrator has himself in a garden surrounded by a high wall. He and the house's owner are unpacking a water pump that had been wrapped in straw for the winter. They hear a scrabbling noise and look up to see a fellow called Sneckie desperately clambering over the wall. From the top, Sneckie drops onto the roof of the henhouse then slides down a board to the ground.

Sneckie recovers his breath and spends a few moments discussing whatever business he had with the house's owner. Then he sighs heavily, looks at the wall, and says he'd best be off again. As he starts climbing, the puzzled narrator says, "Wouldn't you be better using the gate?"

"There's a gate?" asks Sneckie in delighted amazement. He'd first climbed the garden wall as a mischievous schoolboy and was such a creature of habit that, even as an adult, he had never considered any other way. The house's owner had always wondered why Sneckie came visiting that way but hadn't thought it polite to comment on someone else's ways.

Auld Licht Idylls may have been published 120 years ago, but those three characters are still with us. Sneckies still live by habits learned when they were young. They know life is hard and think it pointless—but they just don't see any other way.

Then there are people like the house owner. They know about the gate. They know the gate is Jesus Christ, the One who gives meaning to all our struggles, but they don't think it's their place to tell Sneckie.

Then there people like the narrator—for whom the gate is the obvious way—and they tell folks about it.

Do you recognize yourself in that lot? Do you know the way but let embarrassment stop you from telling others the way to heaven? Or are you one of the brave few who know the way and want to take as many others with you as you can?

Or. . .are you a Sneckie—doing it the way your friends did it, doing it the hard way because that's real and anything else is just sissy escapism; and you're endlessly climbing walls with no hope of anything but another wall?

If you are, for God's sake and yours, use the gate!

*Therefore Jesus said again, "I tell you the truth,
I am the gate for the sheep."*

JOHN 10:7 NIV

For Further Thought

1. What self-imposed obstacles keep you from telling others about your faith in Jesus Christ? Fear? Embarrassment? What steps can you take to overcome those obstacles today?

2. Who are the "Sneckies" in your life? What can you do today to lay the groundwork for sharing your faith with them?

I've read this book ❑

My Star Review ☆ ☆ ☆ ☆ ☆

BLACK BEAUTY

Author

Anna Sewell, 1820–1878

First published

1877

Original publishers

Jarrold & Sons, London, England

Notes

- Once said to be the sixth most popular book in the English language
- The 1971 film starred Mark Lester (Oliver Twist in *Oliver!*)

HORSE SENSE

*I*f animals could talk, what would they teach us about compassion? Anna Sewell wrote the classic novel *Black Beauty*, first published in 1877, intending to promote more humane treatment of horses. The story, uniquely narrated by the horse, models the utmost importance of compassion and kindness by telling about the positive and negative experiences in Black Beauty's life.

The story begins with Black Beauty as a colt. His mother wisely counsels him, saying, "I hope you will grow up gentle and good and never learn bad ways. Do your work with good will. . .and never bite or kick even in play." These words of wisdom provide guidance for Black Beauty's entire lifetime.

One story tells of Black Beauty bringing his master home in the carriage. They crossed a bridge where the river was rising, but his master drove on, for at that time the road was safe. The storm grew worse, with tree branches falling and lightning flashing all around them. Darkness surrounded them on their trip home where once again they approached the bridge.

> *"The moment my feet touched the first part of the bridge, I felt sure there was something wrong. I made a dead stop. . .of course I could not tell him, but I knew very well that the bridge was not safe. Master said God had given men reason by which they could find out things for themselves; but he had given animals knowledge, which did not depend on reason and which was much more perfect in its way and by which they had often saved the lives of men."*

Another story involves a gentleman who spoke up after seeing the horses being brutally whipped and reined in:

> *"I should have thought you had enough business of your own to look after without troubling yourself about other people's horses and servants. Do you know why this world is as bad as it is? . . . It is because people think only about their own business, and won't trouble themselves to stand up for the oppressed, not bringing the wrongdoer to light. My doctrine is this, that if we see cruelty or wrong that we have the power to stop and do nothing, we make ourselves sharers in the guilt."*

Many opportunities to make a difference in this world are around us, if we pay attention and respond as life's ups and downs impact those around us. Choosing to be kind and compassionate is, after all, just common horse sense.

Be kind and compassionate to one another, forgiving each other, just as in Christ God forgave you.

EPHESIANS 4:32 NIV

For Further Thought

1. How do you respond when you see some of the injustices committed against your fellow human beings?

2. What deeds can you do and what words can you speak today—and every day—to extend God's kindness and compassion to those who need it most?

I've seen this movie ❏

My Star Review ☆ ☆ ☆ ☆ ☆

THE BOY IN THE STRIPED PAJAMAS

Author

JOHN BOYNE, BORN 1971

First published

2006

Original publisher

DAVID FICKLING BOOKS, LONDON, ENGLAND

Notes

- REACHED NUMBER ONE ON THE *NEW YORK TIMES* BEST SELLER LIST
- SOLD MORE THAN FIVE MILLION COPIES
- THE FILM WAS RELEASED IN 2008

ONE OF US

$\mathcal{J}$ohn Boyne's 2006 novel *The Boy in the Striped Pajamas* is the story of Bruno, a little German boy whose father just happens to be a high-ranking Nazi officer.

Bruno is unhappy because Father's work takes them away from home to a place, a Nazi concentration camp, where he has no friends. Eventually, through boredom and disobedience, Bruno meets Schmuel, a boy his age who lives on the other side of a wire fence and who wears striped pajamas.

Because he doesn't understand the labels that separate him and the other boy, Bruno eventually comes to see Schmuel as a friend. He even goes under the wire and dons pajamas himself—on the same day Schmuel and the other children are rounded up to be gassed.

But there's another story here. Bruno's father is an important man, and "The Fury has big things in mind for him." When "The Fury" (the Führer) gives Father command of an extermination camp, Mother sighs and tells

Bruno they must go "more than a mile away. Quite a lot more than that, in fact."

Bruno's father is being sent to hell on earth, and he goes there believing it is the right thing to do. But by the end of the story, Father is being taken away by soldiers, probably to face a firing squad. He goes with them and is "happy to do so because he really didn't mind what they did to him anymore."

What made the difference? Well, his son had put himself in amongst an "inferior race" and had died with them. In his last days, Bruno's father must have known what it felt like to be one of "them" as opposed to one of "us." The knowledge came at the price of his son and cost him his life, but it probably pulled him back from the brink of hell to a place where The Fury had no power over him.

The real Fury (Satan) relies on notions of "us and them" to divide us, but God made sure no such hellish idea separated Him from humanity. The agony Bruno's father went through would not have been very different from that suffered by our Father when His Son willingly died amongst this "inferior race."

The message that comes through such suffering is that no matter our race, our heritage, our appearance, we are all God's children. There is no "us" and "them," only "us and Him."

*"For God so loved the world that he gave his one
and only Son, that whoever believes in him shall
not perish but have eternal life."*

JOHN 3:16 NIV

For Further Thought

1. What are some of the ways in which humans today tend to "classify" themselves as "us" or "them"?

2. How should God the Father's sacrifice of His Son for you change how you see those who are "different" from you—different in race, in social class, in any other way?

I've read this book ❏

My Star Review ☆ ☆ ☆ ☆ ☆

CHARLOTTE'S WEB

Author
E. B. White, 1899–1985

First published
1952

Original publisher
Harper & Brothers, New York, New York

Notes
- *Publisher's Weekly* called this the best-selling children's paperback of all time
- Has inspired several animations, a live-action movie, and at least one computer game

SEASONAL WEBS

*W*hen you're a pig, not ending up on the dinner plate takes something special. Fortunately for Wilbur the pig, that's exactly what happens.

In the famous children's novel *Charlotte's Web*, Wilbur begins life as the runt of the litter. He is doomed until Fern, whose family owns the farm he was born on, intervenes and talks her father into letting her raise Wilbur. Once Wilbur is big enough, he goes to live at a different farm, where he meets a variety of animals who become his friends.

Wilbur's best friend, however, isn't a four-legged creature but an eight-legged one. Charlotte is a spider who lives above the doorway of the barn. Their friendship grows as the seasons follow one after another.

When Wilbur learns he could soon be killed, Charlotte pledges to protect him. That's a big promise for a little spider to make, but Charlotte is determined. She sets about spinning webs with messages in them. Her webbed accolades for Wilbur soon make him famous.

His notoriety and his medal at the county fair ensure he will die of old age.

For Charlotte, however, the end is near. When autumn comes, Charlotte builds an egg sac full of her offspring and prepares to die. Wilbur is heartbroken when he learns Charlotte won't be returning with him from the fair. His only comfort is in taking her egg sac back with him to the farm.

After the winter season has passed, Charlotte's children emerge from the egg sac. While most leave the farm, three stay behind and befriend Wilbur. He loves them dearly, but his heart forever remains with Charlotte.

The changing seasons mark the passage of time in *Charlotte's Web*. We also go through seasons, many of which are filled with the different people God places in them. Some people remain for a while, but others pass through quickly like a gust of wind. Some bring us encouragement and joy, but others cause us stress or pain.

Why God places particular persons in our lives at certain times isn't always clear. What is clear is that the seasons we spend beside others will affect our lives—and theirs. So we should make every effort to be a reflection of God's love and to try and see others as God sees them.

Wilbur didn't see a spider when he looked at Charlotte; he saw a friend. Charlotte felt the same. They gave one another the very best they had to give. With God's help, we can do likewise with those we share our seasons with here on earth.

There is a time for everything,
and a season for every activity under heaven.

ECCLESIASTES 3:1 NIV

For Further Thought

1. Can you think of someone who is "different" from you who just might need you to give him or her the best you have to give today?

2. Think back on some of the people God has placed in your life in the past. What kinds of influences did they have on you? What kinds of influences did you have on them?

I've read this book ❑

My Star Review ☆ ☆ ☆ ☆ ☆

CHRISTY

Author
CATHERINE MARSHALL, 1914–1983

First published
1967

Original publisher
McGraw Hill, New York, New York

Notes
- *Christianity Today* listed this as 27TH of 50 influential post-WWII books
- The 1994 TV film costarred Tyne Daly of *Cagney and Lacey* fame

THE UTTERMOST PARTS
OF THE WORLD

Catherine Marshall's best-selling novel *Christy* tells the story of Christy Huddleston, an idealistic nineteen-year-old woman who responds to God's call on her life.

As the story begins, Christy lives in Asheville, North Carolina, and spends her days attending tea parties and making social calls. However, when she hears an impassioned speech by a doctor who has done missionary work, Christy decides to trade in her comfortable life for one of adventure as a schoolteacher in a remote region of the Appalachian Mountains. When Christy leaves her simple life and heads off to the small town of Cutter Gap, she has no idea of the challenges that await her. She is simply doing what she feels the Lord has led her to do and going where He has told her to go.

When Christy arrives in Cutter Gap, she faces unforeseen challenges, and she begins to question both her calling and her abilities. The people in Cutter Gap are not open to outsiders invading their territory, and they make it clear they don't want her there. Most are very superstitious as well. It takes Christy time to acclimate herself, and there are many moments when she wants to turn and run back to North Carolina, where life was easy.

In the end, Christy stays put and falls in love with both the people and the area. She proves that she has the goods to see it through. She also comes to realize that while she came to Cutter Gap to teach, in the end she learned many valuable lessons herself.

Consider Christy's heartfelt words: "When I left my city home to be a schoolteacher at a backwoods mission, I dreamed of adventure. I wasn't ready for the real challenges of life in these mountains. I'd have given up, if not for the children. I came to Cutter Gap to teach, but they show me every day I'm here to learn."

Like Christy, we are called to "go". . .to our workplace, to our children's PTA, to an inner-city ministry, and possibly even to foreign missions. And even though we now have every good thing at our disposal—the World Wide Web, great teaching materials, and so on—the task is still great. As you ponder how you can respond to God's call on your life, remember that the Lord uses both your strengths and your weaknesses to touch others. But also realize that He might just teach you a thing or two as well.

But ye shall receive power, after that the Holy Ghost is come upon you: and ye shall be witnesses unto me both in Jerusalem, and in all Judaea, and in Samaria, and unto the uttermost part of the earth.

ACTS 1:8 KJV

For Further Thought

1. What "spheres of influence" has God placed you in, and how can you most effectively and appropriately share your faith with others who live in those spheres?

2. Can you think of a time in your life when God used someone you wouldn't have expected as a means to teach you an important spiritual lesson?

I've read this book ❏

My Star Review ☆ ☆ ☆ ☆ ☆

THE COUNT
OF MONTE CRISTO

Author
ALEXANDRE DUMAS, 1802–1870

First published
SERIALIZED 1844–1846 IN *JOURNAL DES DÉBATS*
PUBLISHED IN 1846

Original publisher (in English)
CHAPMAN & HALL, LONDON, ENGLAND

Notes
- THE COUNT WAS THE INSPIRATION FOR LEW
WALLACE'S BIBLICAL HERO BEN-HUR
- FILMED MANY TIMES, FROM 1934 TO 2002

POWER AND WISDOM
ARE IN GOD'S HANDS

*I*n Alexandre Dumas's *The Count of Monte Cristo*, manipulative, self-absorbed men wrongly accuse and imprison Edmond Dantès, the story's main character. One of Edmond's malefactors, Fernand Mondego, marries Edmond's fiancée as soon as he is imprisoned. Mondego's partner in crime, Villeforte, agrees to trumped-up charges against Edmond to protect his own tarnished reputation. Edmond's years in prison leave him bitter and vengeful.

A bright spot of Edmond's imprisonment happens when he meets a fellow prisoner, the Abbé Faria, whose attempts to dig to freedom lead him to Edmond's cell. The two form a friendship and begin meeting daily. In the course of their friendship, Faria tells Edmond of a tremendous fortune buried near an island. When Faria dies, his body is placed in a sack to be thrown into the sea. Edmond switches places with Faria's body and works his way out of the sack in the water then swims through the dark water to an island.

Edmond recovers Faria's fortune and vows to use it to exact revenge against those who have wronged him. He takes the name The Count of Monte Cristo and dazzles society with his wealth and grace—all the while plotting the revenge of those who sent him to prison.

Killing each man quickly would not give Edmond the satisfaction he believes revenge should provide him, so he sets up elaborate plots to slowly ruin each man anonymously. Fernand, who had married Edmond's beloved Mercédès, is deserted by his wife and son and shoots himself. Edmond persuades Villeforte's wife to carry out a series of poisonings, and when his archenemy Villeforte finds out, he goes mad.

One of the poisoning victims is Villeforte's daughter, Valentine, a woman Edmond's true friend, Maximilian, loves. Edmond senses his friend's pain, reassesses the damage he has caused, and realizes that the power to punish is not his, but God's. He makes reparation by rescuing Valentine from the verge of death and reuniting her with Maximilian. Edmond finally realizes that he "believed himself for an instant to be equal to God," but now he knows that "supreme power and wisdom are in the hands of God alone."

Dumas's tale winds from unjust imprisonment and betrayal to revenge but ends with one man's realization of God's power and wisdom and man's place in the world. Edmond's happiness comes once he realizes that God is more powerful than man. He is finally able to rest in God's forgiveness.

Do not take revenge, my friends, but leave room for God's wrath, for it is written: "It is mine to avenge;
I will repay," says the Lord.

ROMANS 12:19 NIV

For Further Thought

1. Can you think of someone right now who has hurt you—maybe deeply and maybe in the distant past? How do you think it would benefit you to let go of that hurt and forgive that person?

2. How does knowing that God always looks out for you change your outlook on those who have hurt you?

I've read this book ❑

My Star Review ☆ ☆ ☆ ☆ ☆

CRIME AND PUNISHMENT

Author
Fyodor Dostoyevsky, 1821–1881

First published
Serialized in *The Russian Messenger*, 1866
Published in book form, 1886

Original publisher (in English)
Vizetelly & Co., London, England

Notes
- Filmed more than 25 times
- After one episode, critics called this
Dostoevsky's most important work

New Life

*F*yodor Dostoevsky's novel *Crime and Punishment* is a story of sin, suffering, and redemption. This complex study in contrasts ends with a hopeful message of regeneration for all.

This is no mystery story. The reader is aware of the perpetrator from the beginning. Rodion Raskolnikov, called Rodya, is a brilliant young student who plans and executes a murder. Rodya is unsure of his own motives, and he examines them repeatedly. Robbery cannot be the motive, as he takes jewelry from the pawnbroker after murdering her but hides the spoils.

Rodya has written of a theory regarding two types of man: the ordinary and extraordinary. The ordinary man cannot bring any new thing to the table and is therefore subject to the law. The extraordinary man, however, is above the law. He seems to be challenging his own theory by committing this murder and then testing himself to see if he is extraordinary.

What follows throughout much of the book is Rodya's suffering, as he endures questioning and self doubt. He befriends Sonia, who, ironically, is one of the few characters of faith in this book. Sonia had lived with an alcoholic father and two young siblings, and her stepmother encouraged her to pursue prostitution to put bread on the table. Deeply ashamed of her actions, Sonia is wounded yet strong.

Rodya recognizes Sonia as flawed but as a woman of faith, and he confesses his crimes to her. It is much easier for Rodya to confess to one who has made moral mistakes as well. Her compassionate nature draws him. She encourages him to confess publicly and vows to go to Siberia with him.

Once in Siberia, Sonia leaves behind her shameful occupation and becomes an example of selflessness to all around her. She visits all the prisoners, mends clothes, and helps with letters from home. Rodya eventually sees Christ's compassion reflected in Sonia and asks, "Can not her faith be mine?" Although Rodya has suffered because of his crime, he learns that it is not his suffering that brings new life but Christ's.

Dostoevsky's daughter tells the story of her father calling his children to his deathbed, where he shared the story of the prodigal son. He reminded his children, "No matter what you have done or what awful crime you may have committed, the Father stands with open arms if you will but receive Him." New life is available to all—from the prostitute, the murderer, and the thief on the cross to the housewife and the businessman.

> *Therefore, if anyone is in Christ, he is a new creation;*
> *the old has gone, the new has come!*
>
> 2 CORINTHIANS 5:17 NIV

For Further Thought

1. What does it mean to you to be "in Christ"? How has being in Him affected your life?

2. How would you respond to someone who truly believed he or she had committed too many horrible sins to be worthy of salvation?

I've read this book ❏

My Star Review ☆ ☆ ☆ ☆ ☆

DON QUIXOTE

Author
MIGUEL DE CERVANTES, 1547–1616

First published
1605 (PART ONE), 1615 (PART TWO)

Original publisher
JUAN DE LA CUESTA, MADRID

Notes
- REGULARLY LISTED AS ONE OF THE GREATEST
  WORKS OF FICTION EVER PRODUCED
- IN 1973, RUDOLPH NUREYEV BROUGHT A BALLET
  VERSION TO THE SILVER SCREEN

A TRULY NOBLE QUEST

*P*ublished around four hundred years ago in Spain, the fame of Miguel Cervantes' *Don Quixote* has grown to worldwide proportions. It has inspired imitators, sequels, films, plays, operas, paintings, and sculpture. The unlikely knight is still recognized today.

Don Quixote is really Alonso Quixano, landowner, dreamer, and avid reader. His properties fall into disrepair because Quixano spends so much time reading tales of "knights errant." Despite being in his latter years, he decides to take up this chivalric ideal. He wants to be a hero!

From the start, he deceives himself. His quests will be in the name of great lady—actually a local farmer's daughter he hardly knows. He names his horse Rosinante, which means "no longer a nag," despite the fact it plainly still is. Spotting windmills in the distance, he insists they are wicked giants who must be vanquished.

In sad actuality, Quixote does more harm than good in his quest by refusing to live in the real world. Eventually, his tenants use his delusion to trick him into coming home, where, briefly before he dies, he reverts to being simply "Alonso the Good."

It's easy to get caught up in chivalry and romance. They have a lot to recommend them. But the foundations of Quixote's misadventures were either his own grandiose dreams or his make-believe worship of an unattainable lady—both false gods that lead to him being mocked and repeatedly unhorsed.

The more solid your foundation, the less chance you have of being "unhorsed." God and love might occasionally be mocked, but when you follow them you can't help but do good. With the Creator of the world as your support, who can knock you down?

Wandering the land in search of adventure is all very well, but Quixote had people at home depending on him. We might be fired with the enthusiasm to help others in distant lands, to have thousands hear what we have to say, or to die for a cause. But look around you first. Is there work needing done where you are? Are there neighbors to reach out to, or children to raise in faith? Does an example of God's love need to be set—right where you are?

Let Don Quixote, Sancho Panza, and the other dreamers go on with their endless "noble" quests. In the meantime, God has some *real* work He needs doing, and He needs *real* heroes to do it.

Not lording it over those entrusted to you,
but being examples to the flock.

1 PETER 5:3 NIV

For Further Thought

1. Look around you. Has God placed people in your life—at home, at work, in your circle of friends—who might need you to be their "hero" by just living out and speaking about your faith?

2. Are there areas of life where you believe God might be calling you to be a better example of Christianity? What are they, and what steps can you take to do it?

I've read this book ❏

My Star Review ☆ ☆ ☆ ☆ ☆

THE EMPEROR'S NEW CLOTHES

AUTHOR
HANS CHRISTIAN ANDERSEN, 1805–1875

FIRST PUBLISHED
1837

ORIGINAL PUBLISHER
C. A. REITZEL, COPENHAGEN, DENMARK

NOTES
- TRANSLATED INTO OVER 100 LANGUAGES
- TOLD (AND SUNG) BY DANNY KAYE IN 1952 FILM
  HANS CHRISTIAN ANDERSEN

Fairy Tales or Sound Doctrine?

The Emperor's New Clothes, one of Hans Christian Andersen's most popular fairy tales, introduces a vain emperor who spends all his money on clothes. He never goes anywhere except to show off a new outfit and even has "clothes for every hour of the day and evening."

One day, two swindlers come to town, bragging that they can weave the most beautiful cloth in the world—a cloth so precious that garments made from it become invisible to the stupid and incompetent. Hearing this, the emperor pays the men large sums of money to make him an outfit. They demand the best silk and purest gold thread, which they pocket while pretending to weave on empty looms. Concerned he may not be able to see the cloth, the emperor sends two of his most trusted advisors to visit the weaving room in his stead. Neither sees the material, but both pretend they do for fear of being thought dim-witted.

Finally, the emperor visits the weaving room. But he can't see the cloth either. Certain he must be either dull or inept, he pretends he can. In fact, he praises the spectacular material and makes plans to wear it in a procession the next day. So the weavers, now very rich, spend the night pretending to cut out a marvelous suit of clothes. They dress the emperor in it the next day.

As the emperor parades down the street, the citizens, not wanting to be thought of as fools, cheer loudly and pretend to admire the emperor's new outfit. But then a little child says, "He has got nothing on." The emperor shudders because he knows it's true—but he continues his charade, walking down the street naked.

In this story, the emperor and his subjects allow a pair of swindlers to hoodwink them. Wanting to believe themselves wise and capable (or at least have others think they're wise and capable), they deny the truth for a lie. And the emperor ends up showing just how foolish and incompetent he is by pretending the lie is truth.

As Christians, we have the same choice as the emperor and his subjects. Will we allow ourselves to be deceived by ear ticklers? Will we reject sound doctrine because we think a lie makes us look better? Will we believe lies or cling to the truth as revealed in scripture?

For the time will come when they will not endure
sound doctrine; but wanting to have their ears tickled,
they will accumulate for themselves teachers in
accordance to their own desires.

2 TIMOTHY 4:3 NASB

For Further Thought

1. What are some of the ways the world
    tempts believers to accept faulty thinking
    and teaching and turn away from the
    truths of scripture?

2. How can believers best resist "peer
    pressure" and continue to believe and
    stand up for sound biblical teaching?

I've read this book ❑

My Star Review ☆ ☆ ☆ ☆ ☆

FAUST

Author
JOHANN WOLFGANG VON GOETHE, 1749–1832

First published
1808 (PART ONE), 1832 (PART TWO)

Original publisher (in English)
THOMAS BOOSEY & SONS,
LONDON, ENGLAND, IN 1821

Notes
- THE FIRST ENGLISH TRANSLATION WAS SUPPOSEDLY
MADE BY SAMUEL TAYLOR COLERIDGE
- ADAPTED FOR THE SCREEN THIRTY TIMES BETWEEN
1909 AND 2011

Rely Not on Your
Own Understanding

*J*ohann Wolfgang von Goethe's *Faust* shows the strivings of a man who thirsts for all knowledge and who has an insatiable desire for personal happiness. Dissatisfied with his many years of learning, Faust still desires to know how the universe is held together. In other words, he wants to know what God knows.

Satan, named Mephistopheles in this work, is persuasive and often attractive. He strikes a deal with God in the beginning of *Faust*, receiving divine permission to try Faust's soul. Faust successfully turns Mephistopheles away twice, but the third time he falls prey to the wiles of evil and strikes a deal. Faust declares that if he is able to find one lasting moment of happiness that he wishes to keep, his soul will belong to the devil.

Mephistopheles takes Faust on a number of tempting journeys. Faust finds some relief in emotions such as love, but then he is plagued by guilt when he loses his beloved.

He concludes that man's power should be used in a way beneficial to mankind, and after a series of journeys in which he revisits images of ancient Greece and Helen of Troy, he returns to his vision of usefulness.

As Faust works with others to restore marshy land to a usable state, the sound of work—human achievement—convinces him that he is partaking in a noble achievement. He cries out to the moment, "Oh, stay; you are so fair!" Because of the deal struck with Mephistopheles, Faust falls dead. Mephistopheles moves in to take him away to damnation, but he is confronted with angels and forces of good that instead welcome Faust into the heavenly realm.

Some see Goethe's masterpiece as a picture of universal mercy, as Faust is elevated to the heavenly realm in the end. Others see it as the Romantic expression of the belief in this period that man is naturally good. Still others interpret Faust's ascension to heaven as proof that man's striving toward a noble goal will attain his salvation. Regardless, the poem that culminated sixty years of writing by Goethe is food for thought.

In reality, Faust wanted to know what God knows. He could not accept who he was and trust God for his life and happiness. Faust needed to let go and rely on a God bigger than himself.

Trust in the LORD with all your heart and lean not on your own understanding; in all your ways acknowledge him, and he will make your paths straight. Do not be wise in your own eyes; fear the LORD and shun evil. This will bring health to your body and nourishment to your bones.

PROVERBS 3:5–8 NIV

For Further Thought

1. What does it mean to you to fully and completely trust someone? How does that apply to your life of faith?

2. Are there areas in which you find it difficult to trust God with all your heart? What are they, and what keeps you from trusting Him for them?

I've read this book ❑

My Star Review ☆ ☆ ☆ ☆ ☆

FRANKENSTEIN

Author
MARY WOLLSTONECRAFT SHELLEY, 1797–1851

First published
1818

Original publisher
LACKINGTON, HUGHES, HARDING,
MAVOR & JONES, LONDON

Notes
- MARY SHELLEY WAS JUST 19 WHEN
  THIS NOVEL WAS PUBLISHED
- "THE CREATURE" IN THE 1994 MOVIE WAS
  PLAYED BY ROBERT DE NIRO

SEPARATION ANXIETY

*E*ven though it was written almost two hundred years ago, the warning in Mary Shelley's *Frankenstein* could not be more up-to-date.

Shelley had read about the possibility of reanimating dead flesh, and, in her preface, she explains that the novel might help to "delineate" certain human passions. In other words, "Here's what happens when you play God."

The big question today is, "Just because we can do something, does that mean we should?" For Victor Frankenstein, the answer was a resounding, "No!"

In a time of invention and discovery, Frankenstein sets out to create life. Convinced he is doing good, he imagines "a new species will bless me as its creator."

Frankenstein wants his creation to be beautiful. When, after years of toil, it turns out to be a living, suffering thing, he turns from it in disgust. So begins the separation of creator and created.

The "monster" wants acceptance but gets rejection.

His loneliness and violence inflicted on him in fear help to drive him insane. If he can't be accepted by his "father," he decides, he will destroy everything his father loves.

God never rejects us, but all too often we reject Him. Many are convinced there is no Father—while their hearts still yearn for Him. In frustration and loneliness, we often go too far. Separated from our Creator, we are dangerous beings.

The monster cannot kill Frankenstein any more than we can do away with God, but, in our arrogance, we might easily destroy much that is precious to Him. Things like hope, love. . .ourselves.

Despite attempts at isolation, the man and the monster are inevitably drawn to each other. They taunt and pursue each other all the way to their lonely deaths in the ice of the North Pole.

The monster was a mighty creation, capable of awesome deeds. But, lacking a sense of belonging, he spirals out of control. There is no doubt that mankind, too, can achieve great things (perhaps outstripping even Victor Frankenstein's ambitions), but without the guidance of our Creator, can we deal with the consequences?

Mary Shelley described her book this way: "Frightful it must be; for supremely frightful would be the effect of any human endeavour to mock the stupendous mechanism of the Creator of the world."

If only Frankenstein had reached out in compassion! If only men would accept God!

*Is this the way you repay the LORD, O foolish and
unwise people? Is he not your Father, your Creator,
who made you and formed you?*

DEUTERONOMY 32:6 NIV

For Further Thought

1. God is both your Creator and your Lord.
   But what does it do to your views of God
   to stop for just a moment and think of Him
   only as your personal heavenly *Father*?

2. How does seeing God as Father change
   how you approach Him? How does it
   affect what parts of yourself you give to
   Him?

I've read this book ❏

My Star Review ☆ ☆ ☆ ☆ ☆

GILEAD

Author
MARILYNNE ROBINSON, BORN 1943

First published
2004

Original publisher
FARRAR, STRAUS & GIROUX, NEW YORK

Notes
- IN THE BIBLE, GILEAD WAS A HILL ON WHICH A MAN WOULD GIVE HIS TESTIMONY
- WON THE 2005 PULITZER PRIZE FOR FICTION

GOD'S GOOD GIFTS

*M*arilynne Robinson's 2005 Pulitzer Prize-winning book Gilead is the letter of an aging father to his young son. The father, Rev. John Ames, is in his seventies, in poor health, and expects to die soon, probably of heart failure. His young son, the blessing of a second marriage late in life, is seven years old. Rev. Ames writes with the expectation that his son will be an adult when he reads his father's reflections.

The story takes place in Gilead, Iowa, in 1956. Ames tells the story of his life as a lifelong (except for his years at college and seminary) resident of the small town where, following in the steps of his father and grandfather, he spent his life as a preacher in a small church. Ames loves his town and its people. He views his calling as important, but he approaches it without fanfare. He steadily and thoroughly completes the task of caring for the individuals in his flock. He preaches from his heart every Sunday and has saved written copies of his sermons in boxes in his attic. Sometimes, on nights when he can't sleep, he walks through town praying for individuals as he passes their homes.

Ames writes to leave his son a record of his background and his spiritual heritage. Ames regrets not leaving his son material wealth. The book, a repository of spiritual wealth, touches on family history, relationships, and the truths Ames learned during a lifetime of observing and serving people and studying and loving God. The account is authentic and meditative. Ames writes to record and make sense of his experience. He looks at life in all its complexity, and his experience leads him to deep trust in the ways and words of God. He longs to pass this on to his son.

Many of the expressed truths resonate in the reader's heart. Ames looks candidly at life and then expresses its essence simply but eloquently. He points out real beauty, the sacredness of the sacraments, the wonder of life, the mystery of God, and spiritual realities. The book is slow-paced and leads to reflection—a savoring of the good in life without ignoring the not-so-good.

Ames touches on numerous themes, but an overriding one is expressed in the letter's conclusion: "There is more beauty than our eyes can bear, precious things have been put into our hands and to do nothing to honor them is to do great harm."

*God looked over all he had made, and he saw
that it was very good.*

GENESIS 1:31 NLT

For Further Thought

1. What sort of "spiritual legacy" do you want
    to leave behind after you've gone home to
    be with the Lord?

2. What beautiful things that God has
    created will you stop and pay honor to
    today?

I've read this book ❑

My Star Review ☆ ☆ ☆ ☆ ☆

THE GOOD EARTH

Author
PEARL BUCK, 1892–1973

First published
1931

Original publisher
JOHN DAY PUBLISHING CO., NEW YORK

Notes
- WON THE PULITZER PRIZE FOR FICTION IN 1932
- THE 1937 FILM WON TWO ACADEMY AWARDS

THE GOOD EARTH

The title of the Pulitzer Prize-winning novel by Pearl Buck reveals its main character—*The Good Earth*. The book illustrates the connection between the world God gives us to work and how our lives intertwine with nature.

The story focuses on family and work life in China in the early 1900s. Wang Lung maintains a close relationship with the earth because he produces his livelihood through working the land.

As his values erode and his wealth increases, Wang Lung enjoys the fleeting and deceptive success of the world. The radical changes from harvests to floods, famines, and droughts symbolize the many shifts and unexpected changes life brings.

His fortunes rise and fall as the floodwaters take over his land. Wang Lung continually returns to his intimate connection with the earth, though at times he loses track of his commitment to the earth and its source of renewal and strength. Each time he returns to his deep-rooted calling—to work the land—he finds balance once again.

Even in the end, he turns to his mud hut, knowing it will be his final resting place, which brings him happiness and peace:

> *"Thus spring wore on again and again
> and vaguely and more vaguely as these years
> passed he felt it coming. But still one thing
> remained to him and it was his love for the
> land. He had gone away from it and he had
> set up his house in a town and he was rich.
> But his roots were in his land."*

The earth serves as a powerful backdrop to his daily labor, to the rhythms of the seasons, and to the upheaval and blessings throughout Wang Lung's life. Having his "roots in the land" provides balance and strength for his journey. Though today may look devastating, the land promises hope in tomorrow.

Whether we are digging in our backyard gardens, splashing in the ocean waves, or gazing at majestic mountains, we marvel at the earth. God gave us such an amazing gift. The changing and rhythmic seasons confirm God's reassuring hope and constant love. He is present with us in each new day *and* when darkness covers our world. We are best nourished when we plant our roots deep within God—our good earth.

*The LORD God took the man and put him in the
Garden of Eden to work it and take care of it.*

GENESIS 2:15 NIV

For Further Thought

1. Do you ever take time to just thank God
   for the wonder of creation? Take time to
   consider what it means to you, then give
   Him thanks!

2. How deeply have you placed your own
   "roots" in your God? What should you do
   to go deeper with Him?

I've read this book ❑

My Star Review ☆ ☆ ☆ ☆ ☆

THE GRAPES OF WRATH

AUTHOR
JOHN STEINBECK, 1902–1968

FIRST PUBLISHED
1939

ORIGINAL PUBLISHER
THE VIKING PRESS—JAMES LLOYD, NEW YORK

NOTE
- WON THE PULITZER PRIZE FOR FICTION IN 1940
- THE FILM, DIRECTED BY JOHN FORD,
  WON TWO ACADEMY AWARDS

HUNGER STRIKE

*I*n telling the story of the plight of one Oklahoma family, John Steinbeck immortalized the Great Depression in his Nobel Prize-winning epic *The Grapes of Wrath*.

The bank has foreclosed on the Joad homestead and forced them off land they'd farmed since the 1889 land run. With only a car converted into a truck for transportation, they sell most of what they own at bargain-basement prices. Flyers announce work for all in California. They could eat fruit dropped from trees and get a piece of land to start over again. Along with thousands of others, they escape the Dust Bowl down Route 66.

By the time they arrive in the "promised land," all they have left was spare change and the last of the pork they killed before leaving home. They don't worry, though; they are willing to work hard. The bitter truth hits home as they move from one migrant camp to another. Out of desperation, tens of thousands have traveled west, and now there are more workers here than jobs. Soon, the Joads, along with everyone else in "Hooverville," are starving.

Tom Joad, an ex-convict who broke parole when he left Oklahoma, kills a strike breaker then decides to leave his family before he brings trouble on them. When his ma asks when she'll see him again, he tells her, "Whenever they's a fight so hungry people can eat, I'll be there. . . . I'll be in the way kids laugh when they're hungry an' they know supper's ready. An' when our folks eat the stuff they raise an' live in the houses they build—why, I'll be there."

Sound familiar?

Jesus said much the same thing in Matthew 25. At the judgment, nations will be divided into sheep and goats. The standard of judgment? Their treatment of the Lord. Did they feed Him when He was hungry or give Him water when He was thirsty? Perplexed, they will ask, "When did we see You, Lord?"

Jesus will answer, "When you did it for one of the least of these."

Tom Joad all over again.

When hunger strikes, we must do something to help. Every time we do, we are feeding the Lord.

*"Then the righteous will answer Him, 'Lord, when did we see
You hungry and feed You, or thirsty and give You something
to drink?' . . . And the King will answer them, 'I assure you:
Whatever you did for one of the least of these brothers
of Mine, you did for Me.' "*

MATTHEW 25:37, 40 HCSB

For Further Thought

1. What specifically is Jesus calling His
   followers to do in Matthew 25:37–40?

2. Who are some of the "least of these
   brothers" you can reach out to and feed
   and clothe in your area of influence?

I've read this book ❑

My Star Review ☆ ☆ ☆ ☆ ☆

THE GREAT GATSBY

Author
F. Scott Fitzgerald, 1896–1940

First Published
1925

Original Publisher
Charles Scribner's Sons, New York

Notes
- Second in the Modern Library 100 Best Novels of the 20th Century
- The 1974 film has a screenplay by Francis Ford Coppola

UNWORTHY IDOLS

F. Scott Fitzgerald's *The Great Gatsby* tells of a man in search of an elusive dream. After a poor Jay Gatz meets and is spurned by socialite Daisy, he changes his name to Gatsby and hopes to change his destiny—amassing a fortune through unsavory means.

Gatsby buys a mansion close to Daisy and throws lavish parties in hopes of attracting her. People come in droves to see the mysterious Gatsby and sample all that his riches offer. He is surrounded by insincere flatterers who care nothing for him. Nick Carraway moves near Gatsby's mansion and attends a party out of curiosity, but he comes to sincerely care for Gatsby, who asks his help in reconnecting with Daisy. Nick complies, and an old flame is rekindled.

Daisy's husband, Tom Buchanan, is old money, but he is crude and rude. He has a long-standing affair with Myrtle Wilson, the wife of unsuspecting garage owner, George Wilson. Nick reluctantly tags along as Tom visits

Myrtle, and his dislike for Tom deepens. Later, Daisy, Tom, Nick, Gatsby, and friend Jordan take a trip to the city where Tom's true colors are displayed. He accuses Gatsby of trying to steal his wife and demeans Gatsby's new money. The anger-filled visit to the city comes to an end as the group piles into Buchanan's and Gatsby's cars to return home, with Gatsby and Daisy together in his new yellow car. As the others follow them, they discover an accident near Wilson's garage and learn that Myrtle Wilson has succumbed to a hit-and-run driver in a yellow car. It is assumed that Gatsby was driving, but Nick alone learns that Daisy was behind the wheel when Myrtle was struck. Gatsby's misdirected sense of idolatry makes him willing to take the blame for Daisy should the death ever be traced to his car. Before the police intervene, however, an aggrieved George Wilson visits Tom, who tells Wilson that Gatsby was driving. Several hours later, Wilson and Gatsby are found dead. Wilson shot Gatsby and then turned the gun on himself.

The reader is left with the commentary of narrator Nick Carraway, who tries to plan a respectable funeral. When only a few people show up, Nick's disdain toward the idle rich is confirmed. Nick leaves the Buchanans and others like them behind and returns to his Midwestern roots.

The life of Jay Gatsby serves as a sad commentary on the shallowness of the idle rich and on the futility of chasing unworthy idols, for in the end, there is no other God but one.

We know that an idol is nothing in the world,
and that there is none other God but one.

1 CORINTHIANS 8:4 KJV

For Further Thought

1. What are some of the "gods" this world puts in believers' ways in order to tempt us away from following the one true God with our whole hearts?

2. How can you best avoid the traps the world puts in your way so that you can follow God with everything you have?

I've read this book ❏

My Star Review ☆ ☆ ☆ ☆ ☆

IN HIS STEPS

Author
CHARLES M. SHELDON, 1857–1946

First published
1896

Original publisher
CHICAGO ADVANCE, CHICAGO

Notes
- LISTED AS THE 39TH BEST-SELLING BOOK OF ALL TIME
- FILMED IN 1964 BY KEN ANDERSON WHO ALSO
  DIRECTED *PILGRIM'S PROGRESS*

STEPPING TOWARD HEAVEN

*F*ew would classify the Charles M. Sheldon novel *In His Steps* as high literature. But it's certainly stood the tests of time.

Originally published in 1896, *In His Steps* is still in print through several publishers. At its century point in the late 1990s, the novel generated a boom of WWJD? products and pledges among Christian young people worldwide.

WWJD? stands for "What Would Jesus Do?"—the same question of the story's lead character, Rev. Henry Maxwell. Pastor of First Church of Raymond, a fictional Midwestern city, Rev. Maxwell challenges his congregation to ask what Jesus would do before making any decision—however small or large—and see what difference the answer would make in their lives.

First Church is Raymond's place to be. Its congregation is "the best dressed, most comfortable-looking" in town. With "the best music that money could buy," its soloist, Rachel Winslow, wows the crowd with both her voice and physical beauty—and serves as a perfect lead-in to Rev. Maxwell's sensational oratory. All are pleased to be part of a congregation of "the leading people, representatives of the wealth, society, and intelligence of Raymond."

Then, one Sunday, a tramp shows up at First Church.

The poor, dirty man had stopped earlier at Maxwell's house, only to be dismissed by a preacher preoccupied with preparing his sermon, drawn from 1 Peter 2:21 (KJV)— "Hereunto were ye called: because Christ also suffered for us, leaving us an example, that ye should follow his steps." Having sat through the sermon, the visitor—unemployed and in ill health—asks the pastor and his congregation, "What do you Christians mean by following the steps of Jesus?" After gently denouncing their complacency, he dramatically keels over.

He's not dead—not yet, at least. Shocked into compassion, Rev. Maxwell cares for the tramp in his own home for a week before the man's sickness claims his life. But before that moment, the man thanks the pastor, saying, "You have been good to me. Somehow I feel as if it was what Jesus would do."

The event affects not only Henry Maxwell but also those members of his congregation who take his WWJD? challenge: the beautiful singer, Rachel; her spoiled suitor, Jasper Chase; newspaper editor Edward Norman; heiress Virginia Page; railroad superintendent Alexander Powers; college president Donald Marsh; and several others.

In many ways, asking "What would Jesus do?" complicates otherwise easy, well-to-do lives. But those who stay with the experiment find a new joy and meaning in their existence.

What might asking that question mean to you?

> *Then said Jesus unto his disciples, If any man*
> *will come after me, let him deny himself,*
> *and take up his cross, and follow me.*

MATTHEW 16:24 KJV

For Further Thought

1. How would it change your life if you were to ask yourself "What would Jesus do?" before everything you do or say?

2. Can you remember a time when a simple, unexpected meeting with someone changed the way you approach your life of faith? What happened that day?

I've read this book ❑

My Star Review ☆ ☆ ☆ ☆ ☆

JANE EYRE

Author
CHARLOTTE BRONTË, 1816–1855

First published
1847

Original publisher
SMITH, ELDER & CO., CORNHILL, ENGLAND

Notes
- BRONTË PUBLISHED *JANE EYRE* UNDER THE NOM DE PLUME CURRER BELL
- THE 1943 FILM FEATURES ORSON WELLS AND A YOUNG ELIZABETH TAYLOR

"Forgiveness Is the Mightiest Sword"

*C*harlotte Brontë's *Jane Eyre* follows the life of an orphan who learns the value of forgiveness and mercy. Young Jane, mercilessly mistreated in her aunt Reed's household, is finally sent to Lowood School, where she meets two people who love and believe in her. Helen Burns, a child with deep faith, leaves a lasting imprint on Jane. As Jane rails against forgiving those who have wronged her, Helen shares with her that "forgiveness is the mightiest sword. . . and your greatest reward." Teacher Miss Temple also sees promise in Jane and encourages her, and the love of these two sustains Jane as she grows up.

Jane later leaves in search of her own life and is assigned as governess to the ward of Edward Rochester. Rochester is sometimes brooding but fascinating, and Jane finds herself drawn to him. Just as she falls in love and prepares to marry him, his dark past is revealed. The existence of Bertha, a mad wife locked in the attic, exposes

Rochester; Jane cannot marry one who is already married and feels she should leave Thornfield Hall.

Jane flees across the moor and collapses cold and starving on the doorstep of the Rivers family—St. John Rivers, a clergyman, and his sisters, Mary and Diana. As they take her in and minister to her, Jane forms a bond with the sisters and grows even more. She finds herself drawn to St. John, and he eventually proposes, asking Jane to accompany him to India as a missionary. As Jane is about to accept, she hears Edward calling her across the moor. She returns to find Thornfield Hall a burned-out shell. The fire took the life of Rochester's mad wife, and Rochester is maimed and blind as a result of his attempts to save Bertha. A strengthened Jane finds Rochester broken, and their love is rekindled. They marry, and the closing lines of the book remind us that "once again, God has tempered judgment with mercy."

Jane's sad beginnings remind us that God is the Father of the fatherless. Jane's first exposure to forgiveness comes from her friendship with Helen Burns, an orphan child who knew the Father. Once she is able to forgive those who have wronged her, Jane is strengthened. God's mercy is reflected in Jane's path through life and in her restoration to Edward.

When our eyes are opened to God's working in our lives, we can see how He makes our hardships useful. We learn more about ourselves and others through trying times if we stay focused on Him.

*"For if you forgive men when they sin against you, your
heavenly Father will also forgive you."*

MATTHEW 6:14 NIV

For Further Thought

1. Why do you believe it's so important to God that His people not hold grudges or become bitter with one another?

2. How would you deal with someone who has hurt you intentionally, or who won't acknowledge the damage he or she has done? Would you still forgive? Or would you wait until they confess?

I've read this book ❏

My Star Review ☆☆☆☆☆

THE JUNGLE BOOK

Author
RUDYARD KIPLING, 1865–1936

First Published
1894

Original Publisher
MACMILLAN & CO., LONDON

Notes
- WRITTEN WHILE THE KIPLINGS WERE LIVING IN VERMONT
- THE 1967 ANIMATION WAS THE LAST FILM WALT DISNEY PRODUCED

THE RED FLOWER

*W*alt Disney's *The Jungle Book* is a memorable part of many of our childhoods. Rudyard Kipling's 1894 book of the same name is no less delightful, even if it is a little more red in tooth and claw.

Mowgli is a son of man brought up by wolf parents who know he isn't like them but who love and protect him all the same. When Mowgli is presented to the pack, he needs someone to speak for him. Step forward, Baloo the bear!

It's hard not to draw the comparison between Mowgli and the Son of Man. Like Mowgli, He was brought up by parents who knew He was special and different. And when it came time to announce Him to the world, it wasn't Baloo the bear but John the Baptist.

From early years on, Mowgli obeys the law of the jungle. In his confrontation with Shere Khan, the royal Bengal tiger, it is pointed out that Mowgli "has broken no word of the law," and against him, "there is no fault."

Compare those with Christ's comment on the Laws, "I have not come to abolish them but to fulfill them" (see Matthew 5:17 NIV), and Pilate who found "no basis for a charge against him" (see John 18:38 NIV).

But Mowgli's biggest "crime" is the wolves' inability to look him in the eye. Shere Khan, playing the devil role, tells them Mowgli is shaming them with his stare, and they grow to hate him.

Followers of Christ will come up against hate at some point. People who can't look you in the eye never look to their own behavior for fault. They will accuse the Christlike man or woman of trying to embarrass them. Embarrassment turns to fear, which turns to hate.

How much better would it be if they raised their own game, behaved in such a way they could meet anyone's gaze, safe in the knowledge they walked in faith themselves?

How do we help with situations like that in real life? We could take another tip from *The Jungle Book*. Mowgli defeats Shere Khan by bringing "the Red Flower" to the battle. *Fire.* In a memory of his life before the jungle, he says, "I lay beside the Red Flower, and it was warm and pleasant."

There is a force from before Christ became man that was left behind when He ascended. The Holy Spirit, who has set so many souls aflame, will be your Guide and Defender as you make your way through the jungle of secular wolves.

*"For the Holy Spirit will teach you
at that time what you should say."*

LUKE 12:12 NIV

For Further Thought

1. Read John 16:5–15. What specific roles does the Holy Spirit play in the life of the Christian?

2. Read Acts 2. What happened when the Holy Spirit was poured out on the early believers in Jerusalem?

I've read this book ❑

My Star Review ☆ ☆ ☆ ☆ ☆

LES MISÉRABLES

Author
VICTOR HUGO, 1802–1885

First published
1862

Original publisher
A. LACROIX, VERBOECKHOVEN & CE., PARIS

Notes
- THE 1998 MOVIE STARRED LIAM NEESON AND UMA THURMAN
- THE LONGEST-RUNNING MUSICAL EVER IN LONDON'S WEST END

Truth Revealed

Love and compassion are woven throughout Victor Hugo's tale *Les Misérables*. Disguises and deceptions are central to the plot, but when truth is revealed, characters open themselves up to the love of others.

Jean Valjean, newly released from prison after serving a long term for stealing a loaf of bread, is ostracized because of his ex-convict status. Bishop Myriel takes Valjean in and treats him kindly, but Valjean repays him by stealing his silverware. When the police arrive, Myriel claims the silverware was a gift, thereby giving Valjean another chance at a new life. Myriel's only request is that Valjean become an honest man.

Valjean creates a new identity and becomes quite successful in another town. When Fantine, one of his employees, is fired, he takes pity on her. Learning her plight as an unwed mother with a child in another's safekeeping, he promises to find and provide for her daughter. However, a policeman, Javert, has uncovered Valjean's true identity, and he is sentenced to prison. Fantine dies without ever seeing her daughter, Cosette, but Valjean does not forget his promise. He eventually escapes from prison, retrieves Cosettte from an evil family, and cares for her as a father.

Cosette and Valjean move constantly, always in hiding until they happen upon a convent where they spend happy years. Teenage Cosette meets young Marius in a park and they fall in love, but their efforts to be together are thwarted by Marius's aristocratic grandfather. Marius eventually joins revolutionary forces, convinced that death is preferable to living without Cosette. He is unaware that Valjean has also joined the insurrection, partially to protect the man his daughter loves. When Marius is wounded in battle, Valjean risks his life to carry him to safety, a fact unknown to Marius. After his recovery, all seems well until Valjean confesses his past to Marius, who banishes him from Cosette's presence. Alone and despondent, Valjean simply waits to die. Marius learns the story of his rescue, however, and when he realizes it was Valjean who saved his life, he shares the story with Cosette, and they rush to his side. Valjean dies with Cosette at his deathbed, knowing he is forgiven.

After a life of disguise and deception, the Bishop Myriel's words must have echoed in Valjean's mind. Myriel's only request was that Valjean become an honest man. The truth of Valjean's life—the compassion he showed as he rescued Marius—is the truth that reunites him with his beloved Cosette. Valjean is a flawed character, but he continually chooses love and compassion over revenge, and, eventually, truth sets him free.

"Then you will know the truth,
and the truth will set you free."

JOHN 8:32 NIV

For Further Thought

1. What do you think Jesus meant when He said, "The truth will set you free"?

2. In what specific ways does your life demonstrate the freedom Jesus came to bring you?

I've read this book ❏

My Star Review ☆ ☆ ☆ ☆ ☆

THE LION, THE WITCH AND THE WARDROBE

Author

C. S. Lewis, 1898–1963

First Published

1950

Original Publisher

Geoffrey Bles, London

Notes

- In *TIME*'s 100 Best English Language Novels 1923–2005
- The film won an Academy Award in 2005

THE STORY INSIDE THE STORY

*O*ne of the greatest parables of all time is C. S. Lewis's fanciful tale *The Lion, the Witch and the Wardrobe*. In this unusual story, set during the London air raids of World War II, four siblings are sent away from their home in London to live with an old professor in his large house in the country. While there, Lucy, the youngest, finds a wardrobe in an empty room and turns it into a hiding place. Imagine her surprise when she learns that the wardrobe is a threshold into a whole new world! She steps through the wardrobe into a wonderland called Narnia.

Lucy meets up with all sorts of characters in this strange new place, including a fawnlike creature name Tumnus, who labels her a "Daughter of Eve." He engages Lucy in the strangest of conversations and shares something rather startling: "I had orders from the White Witch that if I ever saw a Son of Adam or a Daughter of Eve in the wood, I was to catch them and hand them over to her. And you are the first I ever met." Tumnus goes on to explain that Narnia is being held captive by the evil witch, who has cast a wicked spell over the land, lasting for a hundred years. In Narnia, it is always winter. . .but never Christmas.

There's only one who can save Narnia from this bondage: Aslan the lion, the one who created Narnia in the first place. Lucy and her siblings meet—and fall in love with—Aslan. They are there with him in the end when he offers his life as a sacrifice to free Narnia's people. And they are there when he rises from the dead, forever conquering the White Witch.

Sound familiar? It should. The real Aslan—Jesus—is the Lion of the Tribe of Judah, the One who laid down His life for us, the One who spoke parables so that people would come to know the love of the Father.

Jesus has taken your life and crafted it into a tale far greater than any parable. In a sense, your life is a story inside a story. There is a nugget of truth inside of you, waiting to be shared with a lost and dying world. Your story—your testimony—has the greatest takeaway of all, because it points people to the eternal Creator of heaven and earth.

Therefore speak I to them in parables: because they seeing see not; and hearing they hear not, neither do they understand.

MATTHEW 13:13 KJV

For Further Thought

1. Do you find it easy or difficult to share your personal story of salvation through Christ? Why is that so?

2. Do you think people see Jesus when they see how you live your life and hear the words you speak? What story does your life really tell?

I've read this book ❏

My Star Review ☆ ☆ ☆ ☆ ☆

THE LITTLE ENGINE
THAT COULD

Author

Watty Piper

First published

1930

Original publisher

Platt & Munk

Notes

- Watty Piper was a pseudonym
created by the publishers
- Based on *The Pony Engine* from 1910
by Mary C. Jacobs

DERAILING EXCUSES

*I*n the book *The Little Engine That Could*, we're encouraged to think we can do something despite the obstacles in our path. The little blue engine that agreed to carry the stranded passengers and load of goods over a mountain is an illustration of perseverance. Little Blue Engine huffed and puffed her way to her goal despite the physical strain. This book reminds us that we can achieve something if we put our mind to it.

Tucked inside this tale, however, is another story. Little Blue Engine wasn't the first engine called upon for help. Three other engines were approached and each one had an excuse for not helping. The first one thought it was beneath him to carry such things as toys, food, and stuffed animals. He didn't want his reputation to be hurt. The second engine was strong enough to pull them, but he was so full of pride that he said no. The third engine said he was too tired.

Then came Little Blue Engine, who was really too

small for the job and who had never been over the mountain. She had valid reasons to say no, but this little engine did something the other engines hadn't: She thought about the boys and girls who would be the recipients of the cargo she'd be carrying. In spite of the difficulties she faced, Little Blue Engine's willingness to serve motivated her to say yes.

What kinds of excuses do we often use when God asks us to do things? Are we the engine that's too tired? Maybe we're the shiny engine and don't want to reach out to those who might "smudge" us and make us seem less appealing. Or perhaps we're the strong engine, bursting with so much pride that we think we only have to serve when, where, and how we want to.

If we see ourselves as one of those first three engines, let's ask God to forgive us for our excuse-making. Let's ask Him to give us a spirit willing to serve, the courage to believe we can do what He's called us to do, and the strength to see it through. With God, we don't have to think we can; we can know we can.

Do not withhold good from those who deserve it,
when it is in your power to act. Do not say to your neighbor,
"Come back later; I'll give it tomorrow"
—when you now have it with you.

PROVERBS 3:27–28 NIV

For Further Thought

1. What is usually your response when someone asks you for help? Do you give it willingly and joyfully?

2. What are some of the excuses people, including some Christians, give for not helping those in need?

I've read this book ❑

My Star Review ☆ ☆ ☆ ☆ ☆

LITTLE HOUSE
ON THE PRAIRIE

Author
LAURA INGALLS WILDER, 1867–1957

First published
1935

Original publisher
HARPER & BROTHERS; NEW YORK

Notes
- THIRD BOOK OF EIGHT PUBLISHED DURING THE AUTHOR'S LIFETIME
- THE TV SERIES SOLD AROUND THE WORLD AND RAN FOR 205 EPISODES

WE'RE IN THIS. . .TOGETHER!

*T*he children's book *Little House on the Prairie*, by Laura Ingalls Wilder, is a classic tale of family love and togetherness. This is evident from the very first words of the book:

> *A long time ago, when all the grandfathers*
> *and grandmothers of today were little boys and*
> *little girls or very small babies, or perhaps not even*
> *born, Pa and Ma and Mary and Laura and Baby*
> *Carrie left their little house in the big woods of*
> *Wisconsin. They drove away and left it lonely and*
> *empty in the clearing among the big trees, and they*
> *never saw that little house again. They were going*
> *to Indian country.*

Do you get a sense of both adventure and love of family in those opening lines? This same theme runs throughout the book. In this heart-rendering tale, Laura shares her journey—both literal and spiritual—as her family moves from their home in the big woods of Wisconsin to a new home on the Kansas prairie—a place where Indians roam and adventures are aplenty!

At the story's onset, Laura is quite young. Still, she is keenly aware of the role her parents and siblings play in her life. With Pa as an ever-present force, the children feel secure. And with Ma around, the girls are nurtured and cared for, even under the toughest of circumstances. The children feel safe under their parents' wings. And how interesting to note that so much of the story is dedicated to the building of the Ingalls home—a place where they can be protected from the elements—a log cabin shelter, which they build with their own hands. In this place, the Ingalls family is ready for whatever life brings their way.

What makes them such a force to be reckoned with? They have each other. They're in this thing. . .together. Together, they brave the elements. Together, they meet new friends. Together, they face heartache and illness. Together, they head off on unexpected adventures. And together, they grow and develop into the people they are called to be.

Who has God placed you "together" with? Your immediate family? Your church body? Think about these people. No, they're not perfect. Not even close. But surely you have weathered a few storms together. You've faced life's challenges, cried tears, and celebrated victories—together. Today, take the time to praise the Lord for both your family and the body of Christ. He has surrounded you with family members—literal and spiritual—so that you will never have to face life's challenges alone. What an awesome Father He is!

Behold, how good and how pleasant it is for
brethren to dwell together in unity!

PSALM 133:1 KJV

For Further Thought

1. Who are some of the closest "family members" God has placed in your life? Think of the things you appreciate most about them and then express your gratitude to God for these people.

2. What are some things you can do to further promote unity and togetherness, both within your earthly family and within your spiritual family?

I've read this book ❑

My Star Review ☆ ☆ ☆ ☆ ☆

LITTLE WOMEN

Author
LOUISA MAY ALCOTT, 1832–1888

First published
1868

Original publisher
ROBERTS BROTHERS, BOSTON

Notes
KATHARINE HEPBURN, JOAN BENNETT, SUSAN
SARANDON, ELIZABETH TAYLOR, WINONA RYDER,
GREER GARSON, KIRSTEN DUNST AND JANET LEIGH
ALL STARRED IN FILM OR TV ADAPTATIONS

LAYING DOWN YOUR LIFE

*A*sk any woman for her top-ten list of classic novels and you just might hear her sing the praises of Louisa May Alcott's endearing story *Little Women*. In this delightful coming-of-age story, the four March sisters face life head-on in the late Civil War era, overcoming tragedies and learning to give of themselves, no matter the cost. Each sister is unique in personality and appearance, and each faces her own set of challenges.

Jo, the second-oldest, is the strong-willed child. She seems to have the most to learn. As a writer and a dramatist, she would prefer to live life through her fanciful stories. However, reality intervenes, calling her to action.

Jo's father—who has been fighting in the war—is injured, and her mother must travel to be with him. The family doesn't have the funds for Marmee's train fare, but Jo has the solution: She sells her long, beautiful hair—her one great love—to cover the cost of her mother's train ticket. What poignant words we read as the scene unfolds:

"As she spoke, Jo took off her bonnet, and a general outcry arose, for all her abundant hair was cut short." Jo has paid the ultimate price for a young woman of that day so that her parents can be together.

As the scene progresses, we see both her courage and her brokenness as she faces the loss of her hair. She wrestles with what she's done, feeling both agony and joy. Ultimately the blessing of her gift outweighs any feelings of loss. There are no regrets.

The Bible often speaks of this type of sacrifice. We are called to give, not just when it's easy but when it is most difficult. And, like Jo, we often have to sacrifice the very thing that is most precious to us, the thing that identifies us.

Think of a time when the Lord asked you to give of yourself sacrificially. . .to lay down your life for a friend or loved one. Was there pain involved? Did you struggle with your decision? If so, did the blessing eventually outweigh the pain?

There is no greater love than to give of yourself for others. The rewards are great, both in this lifetime and in the life to come. And remember, Jesus understands this kind of sacrifice better than anyone else. After all, He gave His very life on the cross so that you might spend eternity with Him. Oh, to understand that kind of sacrificial love!

Greater love hath no man than this,
that a man lay down his life for his friends.

JOHN 15:13 KJV

For Further Thought

1. Just how much are you willing to give of yourself for others? Do you impose limitations on your giving, or do you give selflessly and sacrificially—just like Jesus did?

2. What personal factors do you think keep believers from giving of themselves the way their Lord did when He was on earth?

I've read this book ❏

My Star Review ☆ ☆ ☆ ☆ ☆

LORD OF THE FLIES

Author
WILLIAM GOLDING, 1911–1993

First published
1954

Original publisher
FABER & FABER, LONDON

Notes
- HELPED WIN ITS AUTHOR THE NOBEL PRIZE FOR LITERATURE
- BRITISH "X" RATING FOR THE 1963 FILM MEANT ITS YOUNG STARS COULD NOT WATCH IT

AFTER THE FALL

*T*he characters in William Golding's *Lord of the Flies* experience "the Fall"—the moment when Adam and Eve's disobedience brought sin to humanity—in a literal way, and right from the outset. A group of schoolboys, flying to safety during some unspecified war, crash on an island. With the accompanying adults dead and no rescue likely, the boys soon find themselves facing a basic choice: savagery or civilization?

Like man since the fall of Adam, they choose both, and, also like mankind since then, they go to war over it.

But not immediately. They negotiate, they compromise. Two boys step forward as potential leaders. Ralph wants to build shelters and plan for rescue, but Jack doesn't want to be saved. He wants the thrill of the hunt, the irresponsibility of doing whatever he wants, and the worship of a pig's head on a stick. Because he's powerful, scary, and kills people who get in his way, most of the other boys submit to him. He's wrong, but he's strong, and fear buries their normally decent natures.

They blame their excesses on the Lord of the Flies, the pig's head on a stick. But Simon, a good and decent boy, sees their brutality for what it is: their own nature. So they kill him.

Ralph continues the fight, but he's fighting for what he's been taught is right, not what he feels in his heart. Eventually he takes the pointed stick from under the Lord of the Flies and fights back. As he prepares to kill to live, they are rescued.

An adult appears on the beach. The boys fall to their knees, cry, or hide. Suddenly there are no sides in the battle; they are just boys who did wrong. He's ashamed of them all.

Surely God must see our chosen differences—the things we fight and kill over—as so very childish. The things we justify to ourselves, the things we might like to blame on the Lord of the Flies—these are only important to the devil. They are how he turns us away from our Father, the ultimate adult.

When we do meet God, whether on a beach or elsewhere, we will almost certainly be ashamed of some of the decisions we have made. But let's try to make sure He is not ashamed of us! Let's not be running and hiding like Jack and Ralph. Instead let's be like Simon, already walking toward Him.

"Do not turn away after useless idols. They can do you no good, nor can they rescue you, because they are useless."

1 SAMUEL 12:21 NIV

For Further Thought

1. How do you usually respond when you know you've blown it and sinned against God? Do you tend to hide from Him in shame, or do you run to Him, knowing He is the source of forgiveness and restoration?

2. What biblical promises give you assurance that when you confess your sins to God, you are most certainly forgiven for them?

I've read this book ❑

My Star Review ☆ ☆ ☆ ☆ ☆

LORD OF THE RINGS

Author
J. R. R. Tolkien, 1892–1973

First published
1954–1955

Original publisher
Geo. Allen & Unwin, London

Notes
- In 1999, an Amazon.com customer poll declared this the book of the century
- *The Fellowship Of The Ring* won four Academy Awards in 2001

THE LEAST OBVIOUS CANDIDATE

*T*he most obvious candidate for a hero in J. R. R. Tolkien's *The Lord of the Rings* trilogy has to be Aragorn. He is tall, dark, mysterious, good, honorable, strong. . .oh, and he's a king in self-imposed exile. But instead, we get as our hero a short, squat, hairy-footed Hobbit!

It's the same in the Bible. John the Baptist fits the obvious hero template. Andrew was a handy guy with a sword. Even Judas was up for a fight. Or, if you were betting on outright power, Herod, Pilate, and the Roman Empire should have carried the day. But instead, we are all saved by a defenseless, cheek-turning, self-effacing carpenter's boy.

The Lord of the Rings trilogy (originally planned as one book) begins as magic is leaving Middle Earth. Legolas the elf says, "This should be the time of men—and we shall slowly fade and pass into the west."

The kingdoms of men are many and mighty, but against the rising evil they are doomed to fail—*if* they tackle it on their own. Instead they must put their faith in Frodo, someone who would seem to stand even less chance than they do.

Frodo isn't keen. "I wish the ring had never come to me," he says. "I wish none of this had ever happened." Compare that with Christ saying, "Father, if it is possible, may this cup be taken from me" (see Matthew 26:39 NIV).

And they both go on, seemingly the weakest, least likely ones to save the worlds of men. Both of them believe they will ultimately have to die. And both are tempted— Christ in the desert and Frodo by the continual whispering of the ring. Both are offered the world, if they will but submit to the evil one first.

In the fiery depths of evil's stronghold, Frodo prepares to sacrifice himself before Golem, the living reminder of what evil has in store for us, bites the ring from his hand and falls into the fires. Evil defeats itself.

But Christ. . .He died.

In both *The Lord of the Rings* and in life, man faces evil he cannot defeat on his own. All his works will not overcome. The men of Middle Earth were saved by their faith in Frodo, in love and self-sacrifice.

In this world nothing changes but the name.

I have been crucified with Christ and I no longer live, but Christ lives in me. The life I live in the body, I live by faith in the Son of God, who loved me and gave himself for me.

GALATIANS 2:20 NIV

For Further Thought

1. In this writing, what parts of Christ's character are highlighted? How can you best be an imitator of Christ in these areas?

2. What does the phrase "Christ lives in me" mean to you? How does Christ living in you change your thinking and your behavior?

I've read this book ❏

My Star Review ☆ ☆ ☆ ☆ ☆

MOBY DICK

Author
Herman Melville, 1819–1891

First published
1851

Original publisher
Richard Bentley, London
Harper & Brothers, New York

Notes
- Named Massachusetts's official "epic novel" in 2008
- Gregory Peck played Captain Ahab in the 1956 film

THINE OR MINE

*H*erman Melville lived and worked with Nantucket whalers before writing *Moby Dick*, and it shows. The authentic details make the book a vibrant, exciting read—but it's an older, sadder theme that grips the reader's heart.

Captain Ahab was once a man of faith, but now he is physically and morally diminished. He has a leg fashioned from whale bone, and a facial scar from a thunderbolt. Ahab, who is from a peaceful Quaker background, has come to see Moby Dick, the whale who took his leg, as the embodiment of evil. His response is to pursue the animal with an ever-growing, ever-devouring hatred.

We meet Ahab's counterpart before he and the book's narrator set sail. Father Mapple is another imposing figure—an ex-whaler turned priest, also haunted by his past on the high seas. But Mapple turns away from hatred. The lowliest sinner, he is in awe of a God who can love a man like him.

Like the two aspects of man, the fallen and the forgiven,

Mapple and Ahab are the same but also very different.

At the end of his sermon, Father Mapple refers to the delight of the man who, with his last breath, can say, "I have striven to be Thine, more than to be this world's, or mine own." Then he stays, head bowed in reverence, as the congregation shuffles out.

Ahab, on the other hand, with the conceit of earthly men, thinks himself master of his own fate, even though his "topmost greatness" lies in his "topmost grief." Refusing forgiveness for the creature or himself, Ahab flings defiance with his last harpoon. "From hell's heart I stab at thee; for hate's sake I spit my last breath at thee." The harpoon pierces the whale, but the rope tangles around Ahab's neck—so hate destroys him in the end.

It is in each of us to be Ahab. But we might also be Father Mapple. What makes the difference? Not the lives we lead. Both had similar lives. The difference is what we choose to do with our failings, our crimes, our nightmares. We can stand on our own strength, defying them as they drag us to the depths; or we can kneel and offer them to a God who will deliver us even from the depths of the ocean to a "topmost greatness" of love.

Sink—or rise!

*"Those who cling to worthless idols forfeit the grace
that could be theirs. But I, with a song of thanksgiving,
will sacrifice to you."*

JONAH 2:8–9 NIV

For Further Thought

1. What does it say about our heavenly Father that He could so sacrificially and selflessly love fallen and sinful humanity? What does it say about us?

2. What do you think God wants you to do with your own failings, your own sins, and your own pain? What does *He* want to do with those things?

I've read this book ❏

My Star Review ☆ ☆ ☆ ☆ ☆

NANCY DREW
MYSTERY STORIES

*C*REATOR
EDWARD STRATEMEYER, 1862–1930

*F*IRST PUBLISHED
1930

*O*RIGINAL PUBLISHER
GROSSET & DUNLAP, USA

*N*OTES
- STRATEMEYER'S CHARACTERS WERE GHOSTWRITTEN BY MILDRED WIRT, A.K.A. CAROLYN KEENE
- THE 2007 VERSION WAS THE FOURTH *NANCY DREW* FILM TO BE RELEASED

MYSTERY SOLVED!

Nancy Drew is one of the most popular fictional female characters ever created. Going from one mystery to another, Nancy has been solving crimes from generation to generation, while always maintaining her youthfulness and appeal.

Nancy seems to always be in the right place at the crime time. Whether she's come across a mystery by accident or someone's reaching out to her for help, Nancy continuously uses her detecting skills to assist others. She's tackled everything from a family who schemes to cheat their relatives out of an inheritance in *The Secret of the Old Clock*, to discovering the truth behind the strange happenings at an estate in *The Clue of the Dancing Puppet*.

Nancy's desire to find out the who, what, and why of a situation often causes her to get into some tight jams. Her curiosity has caused her to be tied up, chased, or trapped. Despite the possibility of such dangerous things happening, Nancy just can't seem to keep her curiosity from getting the better of her. Once she takes an interest in a mystery, there's no stopping her from solving it.

It's no mystery that we, like the character Nancy Drew, are curious about people. We may not be looking at them through a set of binoculars like Nancy would, but we see what's going on around us. We're being watched, too. Others are curious about us, especially when it comes to our faith. They're looking to see if we're living out the faith we've told them about. They want to know if we're telling them one thing and then living our lives the exact opposite way.

When their inquisitiveness causes them to look, what do they observe? Do they see us placing our trust in God. . . or wringing our hands in despair when hard times hit? Do these curious onlookers see us handling the pressures of the world while remaining firm in God's Word? Do they hear us admit it when we've messed up, or see us extend a helping hand to someone in need?

Nancy usually didn't set out to discover a mystery; rather she was drawn into it by something she observed. A genuine reflection of our faith will cause those who are curious to be drawn in, thus providing us with an opportunity to share Christ with them.

"In the same way, let your light shine before men, that they may see your good deeds and praise your Father in heaven."

MATTHEW 5:16 NIV

For Further Thought

1. What do you think happens when the light of Christ shines brightly from someone? How do people respond to that person?

2. What do people see when they look at you? What can you do today to make sure they see the light of Christ shining from the inside out?

I've read this book ❏

My Star Review ☆ ☆ ☆ ☆ ☆

THE ODYSSEY

Author

HOMER LIVED SOMETIME BETWEEN 1194–850 BC

First published

POSSIBLY AROUND 900 BC

Original publisher

PRESERVED INITIALLY IN THE ORAL TRADITION

Notes

- THE SECOND KNOWN WORK IN THE HISTORY
OF WESTERN LITERATURE
- KIRK DOUGLAS PLAYED ODYSSEUS/ULYSSES
IN THE 1955 FILM *ULYSSES*

REUNITED

*H*omer's *The Odyssey* details the journeys of Odysseus on his long journey home after the Trojan War. Odysseus encounters monsters who threaten him and beautiful women who desire him, and he is sometimes sidetracked along the way. The wonder in this story is found not only in his wanderings, but in the steadfast devotion of his wife and son as they long for his return.

Odysseus's son, Telemachus, travels to several courts in search of news of his father. Meanwhile, back home in Ithaca, Odysseus's wife, Penelope, is assailed by suitors who refuse to leave the palace. They all vie for Penelope's hand, but she is not yet ready to give up on Odysseus. She promises the suitors she will choose one when she finishes a tapestry she is weaving. Penelope weaves the tapestry by day and unravels it at night to avoid choosing a replacement for Odysseus, ever waiting for him to return.

Odysseus is a focused, strong hero eager to return home in most of the poem. He is determined to overcome whatever hardships are thrown his way and make his way back to Ithaca. Telemachus is the dedicated son devoted to finding his father, while Penelope stands alone at home, patiently unraveling and waiting.

The desire for a reunited home is strong in this work, and loyalty is seen across the board. Odysseus returns disguised as a beggar in a plan to rid the palace of the sycophant suitors, and when an old servant bathes his feet, she notices a familiar scar. Stirred by her loyalty, she keeps Odysseus's secret. Even Odysseus's old dog thumps his tail at his master's return in yet another display of loyalty not dimmed over the course of more than ten years.

Ultimately, Odysseus, still disguised as a beggar, teams with Telemachus in a surprise assault on the suitors who have degraded and defaced their home for so long. At the end, the family is reunited.

How like Odysseus we are! Beset by trials on our way, we are sometimes distracted. Nevertheless, One waits for us at home with open arms. He searches for us as Telemachus did for his father, and His loyalty is unshaken. We will be reunited with Him and His presence will endure forever.

"But while he was still a long way off, his father saw him and was filled with compassion for him; he ran to his son, threw his arms around him and kissed him."

LUKE 15:20 NIV

For Further Thought

1. What should be your response when you realize that you've allowed difficulties and trials—or anything else—to distract you from God?

2. What does God do when one of His children becomes distracted, or even walks away from Him temporarily?

I've read this book ❏

My Star Review ☆ ☆ ☆ ☆ ☆

PARADISE LOST

Author
JOHN MILTON, 1608–1674

First published
1667

Original publisher
SAMUEL SIMMONS, LONDON

Notes
- COMPOSED, MOSTLY, WHILE MILTON WAS BLIND
- AN EPIC POEM ORIGINALLY PRODUCED IN TEN BOOKS

An Epic of Hope

*T*he poetry and power of *Paradise Lost*, written by John Milton in the 1600s, stand unrivaled today. Milton's attempt to Christianize the classic tradition of the epic—to do with a cast of biblical characters what Homer did with his gods and goddesses—is poetic rather than realistic, so to quibble with their scriptural authenticity would be to misunderstand his goal. As we read Milton's words about the realities of the Christian life, we are compelled by good and repelled by evil. We all know the story of the loss of paradise; the value of Milton's version is in his poetic contrasts that lead to an ending of hope.

Paradise Lost is split into twelve books. Milton takes the reader to hell first, with a true picture of darkness. Next is a glimpse of life in heaven, with familiar biblical allusions. Milton next provides a view of life as God intended, in Eden before the Fall. In the next book, he recalls the battle between good and evil and then displays divine creativity in the Creation accounts. Milton devotes two books to an account of Adam and Eve's fall and its consequences, while the last two books look toward the future with hope and consolation.

This epic poem is a wealth of imagery, but its move toward hope makes it inspirational. The last four lines provide a number of paradoxes for the reader to consider:

> *The world was all before them, where to choose*
> *Their place of rest, and Providence their guide.*
> *They hand in hand, with wandering steps and slow,*
> *Through Eden took their solitary way.*

Our vision of Adam and Eve departing the garden with the flaming sword waving behind them is balanced in Milton's poem by an innate hope. "The world was all before them, where to choose their place of rest" implies vastness of choice for Adam and Eve. This could be seen as bewildering, but it is implied that they're on their way to a "place of rest" and that they are guided by Providence. What better way to travel?

Adam and Eve take their "solitary" way, implying isolation of sorts, but we must remember that Providence is their guide, so they never travel alone. In addition, their exit is made "hand in hand"—they have companionship with one another as well as with their Maker. Adam and Eve are moving out into a fallen world as do we, but armed with revelations from Milton and, most importantly, from scripture, we can make that move in confidence and faith.

"You will be secure, because there is hope; you will look about you and take your rest in safety."

JOB 11:18 NIV

For Further Thought

1. Where do you place your security and hope? In your heavenly Father? Or in some*one* or some*thing* else?

2. Do you ever spend time just enjoying companionship with God? In what setting do you think you could best do that?

I've read this book ❏

My Star Review ☆ ☆ ☆ ☆ ☆

THE PEARL

Author
John Steinbeck, 1902–1968

First published
1947

Original publisher
Viking Press, New York
William Heinemann, London.

Notes
- Based on a Mexican morality tale
- Lukas Haas starred in the 2001 film version

WHAT IS A MAN PROFITED?

*F*ew stories have lingered in the minds of readers like *The Pearl*, John Steinbeck's classic tale of gain and loss. In this sobering story, Kino, a young Mexican Indian pearl diver, gains the world—but nearly loses his soul in the process.

At the onset of the story, a scorpion stings Kino's baby boy, Coyotito. The town doctor refuses to treat the youngster, because the family can't afford to pay the physician what he feels he is worth. Juana, Kino's wife, tends to the baby herself, applying seaweed to his shoulder while Kino goes back to work, diving for oysters. One day, he spots an exceptionally large oyster that takes his breath away—and inside, he finds a pearl the size of a seagull's egg. Kino's mind reels with possibilities: Has he found the pearl of great price, one that will change his family's destiny?

This discovery unleashes a chain of events in Kino's and Juana's lives. What is first perceived as a blessing is soon realized as a curse. The pearl buyers conspire against

Kino, offering far too little for his prized possession. Then, in the wee hours of the night, would-be thieves attack him. In desperation, Juana takes the pearl, hoping to toss it into the sea. Kino stops her, though, still hoping the pearl is the answer to life's hardships.

In the end, the young couple faces the ultimate loss. While trying to protect the pearl, their young son is shot and killed. Completely broken, Kino and Juana take the large pearl and toss it into the depths of the sea, realizing it has cost them everything they loved.

Steinbeck himself said of this novel, "If this story is a parable, perhaps everyone takes his own meaning from it and reads his own life into it." Is that true for us? How many times have we longed to gain the world, only to lose our very souls? Like Kino, we head into the waters of the world in search of fame or fortune. But what the world offers pales in comparison to the greater things the Lord has for us.

For those of us who've traded pieces of our souls for worldly treasure, it's never too late to take that "pearl" and toss it into the murky depths. There's only one thing worth pursuing: our relationship with the King of kings and Lord of lords.

*For what is a man profited, if he shall gain the
whole world, and lose his own soul? or what shall
a man give in exchange for his soul?*

MATTHEW 16:26 KJV

For Further Thought

1. What kinds of "worldly treasures" do you think people pursue instead of a relationship with God?

2. What are the "greater things" God offers those who choose to seek and follow Him?

I've read this book ❑

My Star Review ☆ ☆ ☆ ☆ ☆

THE PICTURE
OF DORIAN GRAY

Author
OSCAR WILDE, 1854–1900

First published
1891

Original publisher
WARD, LOCK & CO., LONDON

Notes
- THE ONLY NOVEL WILDE EVER PUBLISHED
- FILMED IN 2009, STARRING COLIN FIRTH

MIRROR IMAGE

*I*n *The Picture of Dorian Gray*, Oscar Wilde introduces the title character through the eyes of Basil Hallward, the man who paints his portrait. Dorian possesses not only extraordinary beauty of face and form, but also the untainted innocence of youth. To Basil's dismay, the immoral Lord Henry Wotton insists on meeting the young man.

Wotton's influence tempts Dorian in much the same way that Satan tempted Eve in the garden. For the first time, he recognizes his comeliness and regrets the ravages time would bring. He says, "If it were I who was to be always young, and the picture that was to grow old! For that—for that—I would give everything! Yes, there is nothing in the whole world I would not give! I would give my soul for that!"

Within days, Dorian meets an accomplished actress, Sybil Vane, and plans to marry her. When the reality of love diminishes her ability to portray it on stage, he breaks their engagement. Later, he learns that Sybil has killed herself.

The next time Dorian looks at his portrait, a cruel sneer mars his previously perfect lips. His dreadful wish has been granted. Almost two decades pass while he pursues all kinds of sensual indulgence. The portrait ages and displays the effects of every evil act. Meanwhile, the face Dorian showed the world remains as youthful and untouched as that of the idealistic young man Basil painted. Public opinion about him is divided; many people shun him, while others can't believe any wrong of someone with such a beautiful face.

Dorian is paranoid that someone will see the portrait and guess the truth. He allows one person to look upon it—the artist. When Basil begs his subject to change his ways, Dorian kills him in a fit of passion. Now, red blood drips from the fingers on the portrait. Yet Dorian's visage remains unchanged.

Dorian Gray enjoyed what many of us dream of: eternal beauty. He hadn't learned the truth God revealed in Proverbs 31:30 (NIV): "Charm is deceptive, and beauty is fleeting." Dorian's charm deceived many, but his true physical appearance, reflected in the portrait, fled as soon as he broke Sybil Vane's heart.

Inward beauty, however, need never fade. Proverbs gives us the key: "fear the Lord." Those who follow this advice will never lose the only grace that counts.

Charm is deceptive, and beauty is fleeting;
but a woman who fears the LORD is to be praised.

PROVERBS 31:30 NIV

For Further Thought

1. How do you think God defines "inward beauty"? What are the different character qualities that make a man or a woman beautiful on the inside?

2. What is the key to building true inward beauty, according to Proverbs 31?

I've read this book ❑

My Star Review ☆ ☆ ☆ ☆ ☆

THE POISONWOOD BIBLE

Author
Barbara Kingsolver, born 1955

First published
1998

Original publisher
Harper Flamingo, New York

Notes
- Selected for *Oprah's Book Club* in 1999
- Kingsolver was awarded The National Humanities Medal by President Clinton

FOREVER CHANGED

*B*arbara Kingsolver's 1998 New York Times Best Seller *The Poisonwood Bible* tells the story of Nathan Price, an imposing, fiercely legalistic individual who is determined to evangelize the Belgian Congo with his version of God's Word. He leaves the United States in 1959—accompanied by his wife, Orleanna, and his four daughters: Rachael, Adah, Leah, and Ruth May—and heads out for a twelve-month mission.

Orleanna and each daughter take turns describing the family's experience. With vivid details and poignant humor, they describe how unprepared they are to live in the jungle and tell of desperate attempts to survive in the alien, primitive culture. They had entered the Congo laden with clothes, cake mixes, and embroidery hoops—intent on passing the stint as comfortably as possible. But the items they carried were useless. They are ill-prepared to secure everyday necessities in the mud-thatch hut village without running water and electricity. Although the villagers initially offer welcome and help, to his family's detriment, Nathan spurns their offers.

Nathan, determined to command the Congolese in the way of the Lord as he sees it, strives to be in charge. He believes the Congolese people are backward and that he can improve them. He doesn't bother to observe or understand the ways of the people he yearns to change. He sets out to force a legalistic, punitive version of Christianity on them. From Day One, his ways destroy his credibility and connections. He declares loudly to the welcoming, scantily clad church members that nakedness is a sin. He repeatedly tries to badger converts to the river to be baptized, not realizing that the villagers avoid the man-eating crocodiles' territory at all costs.

Nathan generates so much animosity that the church votes him out, but he refuses to go. And, although Orleanna and the girls had survived catastrophes like droughts, killer insects, illnesses, and scarcity of food, the political upheaval in the country eventually forces them to flee, leaving Nathan behind.

In the novel, the girls reflect on their experience, each concluding in their own way: *We went to Africa to change Africa, but Africa changed us.*

The desire and intent to change a circumstance, a person, or *even* God through prayer is common. We set our minds and energies to the task but usually come to an impasse and realize we cannot force or finagle change. But we can allow *ourselves* to be changed. God uses circumstances to change our hearts.

"I will give you a new heart and put a new spirit within you; I will take the heart of stone out of your flesh and give you a heart of flesh."

Ezekiel 36:26 nkjv

For Further Thought

1. How should you minister to someone you know needs to change something about his or her character? What part should you play in making that change?

2. What kinds of circumstances has God used in the past to bring about change within you? What were the specific results?

I've read this book ❑

My Star Review ☆ ☆ ☆ ☆ ☆

A PRAYER FOR
OWEN MEANY

Author
JOHN IRVING, BORN 1942

First published
1989

Original publisher
WILLIAM MORROW, NEW YORK

Notes
- FREQUENTLY FEATURED ON HIGH SCHOOL
READING LISTS
- THE 1998 MOVIE *SIMON BIRCH* WAS "SUGGESTED"
BY IRVING'S *PRAYER*

THE LORD FULFILLS HIS PURPOSE

*J*ohn Irving's 1989 novel *A Prayer for Owen Meany* tells the story of best friends John Wheelwright and Owen Meany growing up in a small New Hampshire town during the 1950s and '60s.

The story is narrated by John Wheelwright, years after Owen's death. John considers the life of his lifelong friend, Owen, miraculous and heroic, and he writes as an adult to reflect and explain how Owen's life, beliefs, and words prompted John to believe in God.

John and Owen's friendship is remarkable, given that the major event in the story's beginning consists of unlikely batter Owen hitting a baseball that strikes John's mother, Tabby, in the head, and causes her immediate death. John does not blame Owen for the tragedy. The boys grieve together and grow even closer. Encouraged by Tabby's husband, Dan, they agreed that what had happened was unacceptable, but they still had to find a way to live with it.

Owen is a diminutive individual, so small as a child that the other children his age would lift him over their heads and, in spite of Owen's distinctive nasal protests, carefully pass Owen back and forth. Owen didn't regret or complain about his size or his grating voice quality. He believed that God had designed him and set him apart, that he was God's instrument to accomplish an incredible purpose. He lived anticipating the day he would be called to action.

Indeed, Owen's size and distinctive voice especially fit him for the heroic act in which he sacrifices his life to save the lives of several Vietnamese orphan children in an airport. For his actions, Owen was awarded the Soldier's Medal. John even plays a part in the heroic act Owen completes.

John concludes the book by reminiscing about the game he and the other children had played by passing Owen over their heads. Holding Owen in their hands gave them the illusion of control, but Owen was in touch with, propelled by, and lifted up by a spiritual force that took him out of their hands.

After Owen's death, John frequently prayed two prayers. Sometimes, following Owen's sacrificial example, he prayed for Owen's well-being. Other times he pleaded with God to give Owen back. Although Owen was the cause of John's mother's death, John knew that Owen had given him more than he had taken.

Owen's unwavering belief in a God-given purpose for his life and his sacrifice to accomplish that purpose inspired John to belief and will inspire readers.

The LORD will fulfill his purpose for me; your love, O LORD, endures forever—do not abandon the works of your hands.

PSALM 138:8 NIV

For Further Thought

1. Have you ever asked God to reveal to you His purposes and plans for you? If so, what has He shown you?

2. How do you think a God-given sense of purpose inspires or influences others?

I've read this book ❑

My Star Review ☆ ☆ ☆ ☆ ☆

PRIDE AND PREJUDICE

Author
JANE AUSTEN, 1775–1817

First published
1813

Original publisher
T. EGERTON, WHITEHALL

Notes
- SOLD MORE THAT 20 MILLION COPIES WORLDWIDE
- THE 2005 FILM WITH KEIRA KNIGHTLY WAS NOMINATED FOR FOUR ACADEMY AWARDS

PRIDE GOES BEFORE A FALL

Pride and Prejudice, the acclaimed novel by Jane Austen, has served to remind readers of the detriments of pride for well over a century. In this quaint story, Elizabeth Bennet—the daughter of a country gentleman—is one of five sisters. She lives in rural nineteenth-century England, where a person's place in society means everything. Unfortunately, her family's position is not as high as many, a fact that plagues Elizabeth as the story progresses.

When she meets Mr. Darcy, an aristocrat with an overabundance of pride, she is inexplicably drawn to him. He is quite handsome, after all. However, she is immediately put off by his snobbish attitude. . .and all the more when he intentionally snubs her family. He looks down his nose at the whole lot of them, finding them beneath him. Certainly he is of higher station than she, but why should that cause him to treat her with such condescension and disdain?

Elizabeth reacts to Mr. Darcy negatively, forming a

prejudice against him. This, too, is a form of pride. Through a series of events—both good and bad—the mismatched duo come in contact with each other. Their attraction is undeniable, but there is that issue of pride to consider.

In one dramatic scene, Elizabeth's younger sister Lydia runs off with a young man, disgracing the family. Mr. Darcy rushes in to the rescue, saving Lydia from societal ruin by forcing the young man in question to marry her. He covers all costs related to this venture and even pays off the groom's debts. Elizabeth learns that Mr. Darcy is the family's benefactor and begins to see past his prideful exterior to the person inside and realizes she has judged him too quickly. In the end, Mr. Darcy lets go of his snobbery, and Elizabeth sees him as the man he truly is. . .one with a generous heart.

Even in modern-day society we are taught to be proud—of our country, our families, and our personal accomplishments. We work hard to garner the acclaim of others, and we enjoy being elevated to a higher position. However, pride causes us to think more of ourselves and less of others.

Today, pause to think about the areas of your life where you have been prideful. Is it possible your pride could be causing someone else to stumble? If so, learn a lesson from Elizabeth and Mr. Darcy. Pride does, after all, go before a fall.

Pride goes before destruction,
a haughty spirit before a fall.

PROVERBS 16:18 NIV

For Further Thought

1. What kinds of things do you find yourself being tempted to take pride in? What is it about those things that can make you prideful?

2. How can you best keep yourself humble? In other words, how can you keep your pride in check?

I've read this book ❑

My Star Review ☆ ☆ ☆ ☆ ☆

ROBINSON CRUSOE

AUTHOR
DANIEL DEFOE, 1659, 1660, OR 1661–1731

FIRST PUBLISHED
1719

ORIGINAL PUBLISHER
W. TAYLOR, LONDON

NOTES
- A CANDIDATE FOR THE HONOR OF BEING THE FIRST ENGLISH NOVEL
- THE 1997 FILM STARS PIERCE BROSNAN AS ROBINSON CRUSOE

NEVER CAST AWAY

*W*hen Daniel Defoe wrote *Robinson Crusoe*, he probably never dreamed how this character would capture the imagination of its readers. Crusoe was born in York, England in 1632 and lived with his loving parents. His father wanted him to study law, but Crusoe wanted to sail the open seas and see the world. Without giving thought to what God would have him do, or the hurt his parents would suffer, Crusoe ran away.

Crusoe would make several journeys over the next few years. His first trip ended with his ship sinking. The next trip was more successful, but the one after that wasn't. Crusoe was attacked by pirates and made a slave. When he finally escaped, Crusoe settled down for a time. But it didn't last long; he soon set sail on a trip that would forever change his life.

This time a great storm descended upon his ship, and when it was over Crusoe was the only one of the crew who had survived. He ended up on an island alone, with only a few supplies that he managed to salvage from the ship.

Crusoe spent the next twenty-three years on the island with no human companionship. Finally, a group of people showed up on his island, but not the kind of people who would offer Crusoe rescue. They had come to kill and eat their two prisoners. Crusoe helped one of the victims escape and named him Friday. They became close friends. After spending twenty-eight years on the island, Robinson Crusoe and Friday were finally rescued. Crusoe returned to England with his faithful friend, Friday, beside him.

Friday was not the first one to show himself faithful to Crusoe. God was the first. During his initial year on the island, Crusoe understood that he survived only because of God. Crusoe believed that God had delivered him, forgiven him, disciplined him, provided for him, and blessed him. Even when Crusoe suffered depression, fear, illness, or guilt that he hadn't been following God as he should, he knew God had faithfully remained with him.

Sometimes life can make us feel like we've washed up on a deserted island and are alone. When that happens, we must remember those are just feelings. The truth is that God *is* with us. Robinson Crusoe may have been a castaway on an island, but he was never cast away from God. Neither are we.

The LORD Almighty is with us;
the God of Jacob is our fortress.

PSALM 46:11 NIV

For Further Thought

1. What do you usually do when you feel alone, when God seems completely distant from you?

2. Do you believe there are times when loneliness—at least being away from other people—can be a good thing? Why or why not?

I've read this book ❏

My Star Review ☆ ☆ ☆ ☆ ☆

ROMEO AND JULIET

Author
WILLIAM SHAKESPEARE, 1564–1616

First published
1597

Original publisher
JOHN DANTER, LONDON

Notes
- ONE OF THE MOST POPULAR PLAYS FROM POSSIBLY THE WORLD'S GREATEST WRITER
- FILMED COUNTLESS TIMES, FROM THE BIRTH OF THE MOVIES TO THE PRESENT DAY

A More Perfect Love

*A*t the mention of the characters Romeo and Juliet, we think of love, sweet sighs, and hearts and flowers. But Shakespeare's classic tale *Romeo and Juliet* also reminds us of the folly of young love, the tragedy of haste, and the far-reaching effects of hate. His work underscores the fact that human love can only point to the more perfect love.

At the beginning of the play, Romeo is portrayed as lovesick over Rosaline, a young lady who does not love him back. Romeo has shut out the world because Rosaline loves another. He is not able to function because of his grief. Once he lays eyes on Juliet, however, his affections are quickly transferred. "Oh, she doth teach torches to burn bright," he declares, and claims, "I ne'er saw true beauty till this night." Juliet, too, is quickly taken with Romeo, and, before the night is out, she pledges to wed him the next day.

The next day! Speaking of haste! This is definitely a whirlwind courtship. The entire play takes place over the span of about four days.

Romeo and Juliet both have mentors in the characters of Friar Lawrence and Nurse, and their advice is sometimes wise, sometimes imprudent. Regardless, Friar Lawrence gives the most sage advice of the play when he cautions Romeo, "Wisely and slow; they stumble that go fast." Romeo does not heed this advice, though, and events tumble from there.

The most pervasive message of the play, however, is the far-reaching effects of hate. The Montagues, Romeo's family, and the Capulets, Juliet's clan, have been embroiled in a senseless feud from time immemorial. The effects of this hatred are so far-reaching that innocent citizens of Verona have been killed in the feud-fueled street fights; an entire town has paid for the hatred of a few. This family hatred hinders Romeo and Juliet's love and adds to their hasty, secret path to the altar.

Shakespeare's play ultimately provides reconciliation, but at great cost. The loss of a youth from each family is the price exacted for this resolution, not to mention the loss of other family members in the course of the play. As the play ends, the Montagues and the Capulets pledge to erect golden statues of each other's child and vow to remember the lessons learned through their loss.

Hate is a pervasive emotion, and its antidote is found when we love as Christ loved. If we place ourselves in the center of His love, we not only live the antithesis of senseless hate, we find a wealth of wisdom accessible to us through Him and His Word.

"Love one another. As I have loved you,
so you must love one another."

JOHN 13:34 NIV

For Further Thought

1. What action should you take when you find
   yourself angry or bitter—or even hateful—
   toward another person?

2. What are some practical steps you can take
   to personally and effectively love other
   believers the way Jesus has loved you and
   them?

I've read this book ❑

My Star Review ☆ ☆ ☆ ☆ ☆

ROOTS

Author
ALEX HALEY, 1921–1992

First published
1976

Original publisher
DOUBLEDAY, NEW YORK

Notes
- EARNED A PULITZER PRIZE SPECIAL AWARD IN 1977
- THE 12-HOUR TV MINISERIES WON NINE EMMYS

UP IN THE SKY

Roots, the breakthrough book about an African American family, was published a year before the miniseries that made television history in 1977.

In *Roots*, author Alex Haley traces his family's roots from Kunta Kinte, an African captured by slave traders and brought to America, to himself. A proud man, Kinte clung to his sense of self, including his faith and his birth name. He sought to escape slavery four times. At last, he found love and married Belle Waller. Together, they had one child.

When his daughter was born, Kinte promised Belle he would not try to run away again. He took his daughter out under the night sky and whispered her name in her ear: "Kizzy," which meant "stay put." After naming her, Kinte lifted the infant above his head and declared, "Behold, the only thing greater than yourself!" He was honoring a tradition brought from Africa.

Kinte understood his place in the universe, and he

gave his daughter the most precious gift he could. No matter what the law said or how society viewed her, she was made in God's image. He succeeded; Kizzy longed for freedom, and her son, "Chicken" George, lived to see emancipation. Generations later, a young Alex Haley bemoaned the fact he wasn't there to repeat the ceremony with his firstborn.

While many cultures celebrate a child's naming, few do it with the panache of Kunta Kinte. We can pass on some important lessons to our children from his simple act with his daughter.

"Behold, the *only thing* greater than yourself!" Kinte didn't mean the sky, of course. He meant the Creator the heavens pointed to. Of all God's creation, man is the apex, the one meant to subdue the earth and take care of it. Mankind is unique.

"Behold, the only thing *greater than* yourself." The second lesson is even more important. There is something— or Some*one*—greater than ourselves. All of nature—be it the starry sky, fathomless ocean, or majestic mountain— shouts His praise.

The next time we look at the night sky, let's remember Kunta Kinte's admonition.

When I look at the night sky and see the work of your fingers...
what are mere mortals that you should think about them,
human beings that you should care for them?
Yet you made them only a little lower than God
and crowned them with glory and honor.

PSALM 8:3–5 NLT

For Further Thought

1. As a Christian, in what—or in whom—do you place your sense of identity?

2. Can you remember the last time you looked at the wonders of nature and pondered the greatness of God—as well as your own smallness? What were your thoughts at that time?

I've read this book ❏

My Star Review ☆ ☆ ☆ ☆ ☆

A SCANDAL IN BOHEMIA

AUTHOR

SIR ARTHUR CONAN DOYLE, 1859–1930

FIRST PUBLISHED

1891

ORIGINAL PUBLISHER

STRAND MAGAZINE, LONDON

NOTES

- THE FIRST OF 56 SHERLOCK HOLMES SHORT STORIES
- THE PILOT EPISODE OF *HOUSE* (A KIND OF MEDICAL DETECTIVE) HAS SIMILARITIES TO *SCANDAL*

ELEMENTARY EDUCATION

*E*lementary, my dear Watson." Is there any phrase we associate more closely with Sherlock Holmes?

Sir Arthur Conan Doyle never used those exact words, yet they capture the spirit of the master/disciple relationship between Holmes and Watson. Holmes's brilliance shone all the more brightly against Watson's density.

The case *A Scandal in Bohemia* marks the third time the two men work together. Early in the story, Holmes instructs Watson in his elementary methods.

Watson makes an unannounced visit to 221B Baker Street. Holmes deduces several things from his appearance: His friend has returned to private medical practice, his clothing has been soaked recently, and he has a poorly trained housemaid.

As usual, Watson wonders how Holmes has arrived at his accurate conclusions. The detective explains that the gouge marks on Watson's boots gave the details away.

Watson expostulates. His eyes are as good as Holmes's,

so why can't he practice the same methods?

Holmes repeats a phrase that expounds on his methodology: "You see, but do not observe." He challenges Watson to test his hypothesis. Can the doctor name how many steps led to Holmes's flat?

No, he can't, not any more than he can deduce the character of the person who sent Holmes an urgent letter. He can guess that the man was well-to-do; Holmes knows his nationality and rank. Watson never grew any better at adopting Holmes's methods before the detective's faked death at Reichenbach Falls and his subsequent return. How can Holmes's acolyte observe his methods for so long, yet fail to understand and imitate them?

As disciples of Christ, we fall victim to the same mistake. He modeled the life God calls us to live; we have the record in the Bible. He shares His tools with us—His Word and the Holy Spirit.

In spite of these advantages, we often don't get past the elementary stage. We fail to go beyond kindergarten in the school of becoming like Christ. The writer of Hebrews says we still need milk and elementary truths about our salvation, and that we don't move on to solid food.

Only when we complete our elementary education will we be ready to not only see but also to observe, and to distinguish good from evil.

You need someone to teach you the elementary truths of God's word all over again. You need milk, not solid food! . . . But solid food is for the mature, who by constant use have trained themselves to distinguish good from evil.

HEBREWS 5:12, 14 NIV

For Further Thought

1. Why do you think God gave us the record of His interactions with humans we call the Bible? What should our response be to such a gift?

2. How often do you read or study your Bible? What do you think are the benefits of memorizing Bible passages or taking time to meditate—or deeply ponder—on them?

I've read this book ❏

My Star Review ☆ ☆ ☆ ☆ ☆

THE SCREWTAPE LETTERS

Author
C. S. Lewis, 1898–1963

First published
1942

Original publisher
Geoffrey Bles, London

Notes
- Dedicated to J. R. R. Tolkein
- The company behind the *Narnia* movies plans to film *The Screwtape Letters*

WHO WROTE YOUR LETTER?

*F*or almost seventy years, C. S. Lewis's *The Screwtape Letters* has inspired people with its thought-provoking format. In the book, an older demon, Screwtape, writes thirty-one letters to his nephew, Wormwood.

Wormwood is inexperienced when it comes to bringing humans to the devil, and he has been assigned a new Christian. Screwtape becomes his mentor in teaching him the various techniques to deceive and draw the victim away from God. He shows Wormwood the devil's best tools of distraction and confusion.

Screwtape advises Wormwood to do all he can to keep the young man from prayer. If he has to pray, Screwtape says, then misdirect him to "turn his gaze away from Him towards themselves. Keep them watching their own minds and trying to produce feelings there by as the action of their wills."

Screwtape creates distance between God and humans by encouraging Christians to think of God as located "up and to the left at the corner of the bedroom ceiling or in the crucifix on the wall. But whatever the nature of the composite object, you must keep him praying to it—to the thing that he has made, not to the Person who has made him."

Lewis paints a true view of the differences between God and the devil: "We [the demons] want cattle who can finally become food; He wants servants who can finally become sons. We want to suck in; He wants to give out. We are empty and would be filled; He is full and flows over."

The book makes us wonder what type of letter would be written about our Christian walk. How is the devil deceiving and confusing us?

Life is full of temptations. We often take the wrong turn and hit detours on our path to God. We take our eyes from Him and focus on our problems instead. Yet God is faithful and always ready to take us back into His forgiving arms.

Lewis's unique approach of using letters from the devil highlights ways Satan distracts our attention from God. But God takes this strategy a huge step further when He creates letters written not just on paper but on our hearts. God sends His Spirit into our hearts so we become letters from Him, not from the devil.

You show that you are a letter from Christ,
the result of our ministry, written not with ink
but with the Spirit of the living God, not on tablets
of stone but on tablets of human hearts.

2 CORINTHIANS 3:3 NIV

For Further Thought

1. What story does what is written tell them
   about the God you love and serve?

2. What can you do to make the letter God
   has written on your heart easier for people
   around you read and respond to?

I've read this book ❑

My Star Review ☆ ☆ ☆ ☆ ☆

SILAS MARNER

Author
GEORGE ELIOT, 1819–1880

First published
1861

Original publisher
WILLIAM BLACKWOOD & SONS,
EDINBURGH AND LONDON

Notes
- GEORGE ELIOT'S REAL NAME WAS
MARY ANNE EVANS
- STEVE MARTIN'S FILM *A SIMPLE TWIST OF FATE*
WAS BASED ON *SILAS MARNER*

REDEEMED BY LOVE

Silas Marner, George Eliot's fable of rebirth, tells the story of one man's redemption and another's defeat. Silas, a weaver by trade, lives as a recluse and carries a mysterious past. Wrongly accused of a theft in another town, Silas hoards the money he makes weaving, counting it every night. After years of weaving, his eyesight has deteriorated so badly that he can only see very bright objects.

Silas's contrast is found in a man named Godfrey Cass, who appears to be respectable and upstanding but harbors secrets that destroy his life. No one but Godfrey knows of his drunken marriage and the child that resulted. Godfrey's brother, Dunstan, is plagued with gambling debts and steals Silas's gold one night. He rides headlong into an abandoned quarry and is killed. The town becomes preoccupied with the disappearance of not only Silas's gold but of Dunstan Cass.

One snowy night, a young woman stumbles through the forest and spies Silas's empty cabin. When Silas returns, he sees the glimmer of gold near his fireplace and mistakes it for his stolen wealth. As he nears the fire, he realizes the gleam is the golden hair of a sleeping child. Following footsteps through the snow, he finds her dead mother. Unbeknownst to all but Godfrey, the woman is Godfrey's wife, and the golden-haired child is his daughter. To claim her now would cost Godfrey his respectable name, so he remains silent. Silas takes care of the child, Eppie, and learns to love her. She brings Silas out of himself and he becomes a warm, welcoming figure in the town. No longer the town hermit, Silas connects with those around him.

After years of childlessness, Godfrey decides to reveal to his wife the existence of his daughter in an effort to reclaim her. Silas unselfishly steps aside to allow Eppie to reclaim her father and the wealth that would follow, but Eppie chooses for Silas to remain the father of her heart. Godfrey's harbored secrets tainted his life; even though he was perceived as respectable, things are not always as they seem. Eliot teaches us a lesson through Silas, who learned the true measure of wealth as he was redeemed by love.

We, too, are redeemed by love, an eternal love. Christ's love brings us out of ourselves into a community of believers. We learn to value others more than ourselves, and, ultimately, we learn that all that glitters is not gold. Value is found not among the high-born, but in the rough, nail-scarred hands of a simple carpenter.

My lips will shout for joy when I sing praise to you—I,
whom you have redeemed.

PSALM 71:23 NIV

For Further Thought

1. What kinds of changes has Christ's love made in your living and in your thinking?

2. How can you best share the love of Christ, not just with other believers but also with those who are "outside the fold"?

I've read this book ❏

My Star Review ☆ ☆ ☆ ☆ ☆

THE SECRET GARDEN

Author
Frances Hodgson Burnett, 1849–1924

First published
Serialized in *The American Magazine*, 1910.
Published in 1911.

Original publisher
Frederick A. Stokes, New York
Heinemann, London

Notes
- A 2009 BBC list of "Books You Should Read" included *The Secret Garden*
- The first of many film versions appeared in 1919

WALKING STRONG AND STEADY
WITH FATHER

*I*n *The Secret Garden*, Frances Hodgson Burnett tells about Mary Lennox, a sour, plain-looking girl who travels from India to England after her parents die. She moves to her uncle's manor, but he stays away for long periods because of his grief over his deceased wife. Mary meets Dickon, a full-of-life animal charmer, and Ben Weatherstaff, an opinionated old gardener, and she soon learns the value of playing in the fresh air and working in a secret garden she finds.

Mary grows stronger and healthier over the next weeks, until, one stormy night, she hears crying. She discovers her cousin, Colin, son of the manor lord, whose mother died when he was a baby. He has spent his young life in fear of developing a crooked back, like his father had. He lies in bed, sulky and spoiled, refusing to go outside for fear that someone might see him.

But Mary brings him life. She tells him he's not dying and convinces him to come to the secret garden with her.

Before long, the young invalid abandons his wheelchair and starts walking, working in the garden, and playing with his new friends. But he keeps his strength a secret from the staff because he doesn't want them to summon his father home with news that he is well. He wants to tell the good news himself. Colin's favorite thought is "imagining what his father would look like when he saw that he had a son who was as straight and strong as other fathers' sons."

One day, Colin's father returns to find Colin racing with Mary in the secret garden. He can't believe his eyes: The son he thought was dying thrives, and the garden he thought was lifeless flourishes. And Colin gets his dearest wish: to walk beside his father, "as strongly and steadily as any boy in Yorkshire."

As Christians, we can learn from Colin. We should work not to be weak and frail in our faith. We should strive to grow strong through the spiritual fresh air and sunshine of prayer, corporate worship, and fellowship with other believers. We must nourish our soul with plenty of "meat" from the Word and get our spiritual exercise by doing the good works God calls us to do.

Then when Christ returns or calls us home, we'll be ready to walk strong and steady beside our heavenly Father.

Discipline yourself for the purpose of godliness;
for bodily discipline is only of little profit, but godliness
is profitable for all things, since it holds promise for the
present life and also for the life to come.

1 TIMOTHY 4:7–8 NASB

For Further Thought

1. Do you consider yourself a strong and growing believer, a weak and frail believer, or something in between? Why do you see yourself that way?

2. What kinds of "spiritual self-discipline" do you think should soon become a part of your walk of faith?

I've read this book ❑

My Star Review ☆ ☆ ☆ ☆ ☆

SOPHIE'S CHOICE

Author
WILLIAM STYRON, 1925–2006

First published
1979

Original publisher
RANDOM HOUSE, NEW YORK

Notes
- WON THE NATIONAL BOOK AWARD
  FOR FICTION IN 1980
- MERYL STREEP WON AN ACADEMY AWARD
  FOR HER PORTRAYAL OF SOPHIE

THE BRIGHT MORNING STAR

*W*illiam Styron's novel *Sophie's Choice* begins and ends with rebirth. Sophie, an Auschwitz survivor, has come to America to find a new life, but she is still hopelessly mired in the death she has seen—and the death she feels responsible for.

Unable to truly move on, she attaches herself to Nathan, a handsome and intelligent but psychotic man who epitomizes the Nazi dichotomy.

Like the Nazis in the book (and, often, like too many people in real life), Sophie, Nathan, and Stingo, the narrator, have known God but have rejected Him. In their world, where there is no redemption, a superficially wonderful existence rapidly becomes a living hell.

While her new life lurches to its inevitable collapse, the infatuated Stingo pieces together Sophie's experiences in war-ravaged Europe. Despite being the Aryan-looking, German-speaking, Catholic daughter of a Nazi sympathizer, Sophie falls inexorably toward Auschwitz. There she must make the choice that haunts her for the remainder of her life. Along the way, she faces a series of "lesser" choices that might help lift her heavenward. But each time, she submits to fear and the apparent protection of evil—while others sacrifice themselves for a greater good.

This dependence on evil convinces Sophie she is inherently bad and beyond saving. Stingo tries to help her begin again, but, being morally bankrupt himself, he has little to offer. As Sophie runs knowingly toward her destruction in Nathan's arms, the heartbroken Stingo turns to the Bible for consolation.

Committing suicide in the same method many of her former torturers used to commit murder—sodium cyanide— a hopeless Sophie dies to the strains of "Jesu, Joy of Man's Desiring."

Obliterating his own pain with booze, Stingo falls asleep on a beach, dreaming he is being buried. Waking in the morning, he discovers that children have covered him with sand. Rising from his temporary tomb, the first thing he sees is Venus, the Morning Star.

In our fear that God might not be there, we lash out at the world—and the devil lends strength to our tantrums. But it is we who leave God, not the other way around. Even in the darkest places, His hand reaches out. To take it or not was always Sophie's choice—just like it is for each of us.

And we have the word of the prophets made more certain,
and you will do well to pay attention to it, as to a light
shining in a dark place, until the day dawns and the
morning star rises in your hearts.

2 PETER 1:19 NIV

For Further Thought

1. What are some of the reasons God can
    seem distant?

2. Can you remember the last time you felt
    that God was distant from you? How did
    you respond?

I've read this book ❏

My Star Review ☆ ☆ ☆ ☆ ☆

THE STRANGE CASE OF DR. JEKYLL AND MR. HYDE

AUTHOR
ROBERT LOUIS STEVENSON, 1850–1894

FIRST PUBLISHED
1886

ORIGINAL PUBLISHER
LONGMANS, GREEN & CO., LONDON

NOTES
- APPEARED ON STAGE IN LONDON AND BOSTON WITHIN A YEAR OF PUBLICATION
- THE *NUTTY PROFESSOR* FILMS WERE LOOSELY BASED ON STEVENSON'S STORY

THE STRANGE CASE
OF YOU AND ME

*F*or a story to be filmed more than a hundred times, it must have something to say. Robert Louis Stevenson's 1886 novella *The Strange Case of Dr. Jekyll and Mr. Hyde* speaks to the very nature of mankind.

A fallen being like the rest of us, Dr. Henry Jekyll is fascinated by the dual aspects of his nature. A successful and respected doctor, he has for years been hiding the less benevolent aspects of his personality. He's no better or worse than most of us, but he has the means to do something about his situation. Curiosity makes him wonder what a good man would be like unencumbered by evil, and what the bad would be like unfettered by goodness.

He is convinced his good side, having been exercised the most, will be dominant. After chemically transforming himself into Mr. Edward Hyde, he thinks his hypothesis holds true. Mr. Hyde is smaller, younger, seemingly dependant on Jekyll. But evil only has one master.

Hyde's excesses, which Jekyll delights in at first, feed on themselves until murder is committed. The twin aspects become implacable but inseparable enemies.

In his final hour of humanity, Jekyll contains Hyde and leaves proof of their guilt. Unprotected, and with the forces of justice at his door, Hyde takes his own life.

Stevenson draws London as a foggy city, empty of all but protagonists and victims. A lonely place to face your demons. Ironically, Dr. Jekyll is not short of friends. His lawyer, his best friend, and even his household staff try to save him, but evil starts by cutting people off from the light, and Jekyll cannot ask for help.

The seed of a Mr. Hyde exists in all of us. It has since the serpent tempted Eve. Dr. Jekyll set it free with science but the devil doesn't need any such help. And there is no living with him.

The Strange Case of Dr. Jekyll and Mr. Hyde reminds us what even the best of us—even those of us others turn to for guidance—have in us. That's why we need the church, house groups, Bible studies, etc. We each shine the light of what faith we have on the other. When our faith is weak, others dispel that "London fog." When they are weak, we return the favor. In the light of love, the Henry Jekyll in us remains curious but safe, and Edward Hyde fades away with the ever-decreasing shadows.

*"For where two or three come together in my name,
there am I with them."*

MATTHEW 18:20 NIV

For Further Thought

1. What benefits have you found in your personal walk of faith in fellowshipping with other believers at church, small groups, Bible studies, and other gatherings?

2. How would you answer a fellow believer who told you he or she didn't need to attend church/Bible study/small group in order to be a Christian?

I've read this book ❑

My Star Review ☆ ☆ ☆ ☆ ☆

THE STREET LAWYER

Author
John Grisham, born 1955

First published
1998

Original publisher
Bantam Books, New York
Century, London

Notes
- Reached Number 1 on the *New York Times* Best Seller List
- Filmed by ABC for television in 2003

NURTURING COMPASSION

*O*ne soul-searching instance changed the life of Michael Brock, a self-absorbed lawyer in John Grisham's *The Street Lawyer*. In a flash, Brock's life turns upside down, and he begins to see people he previously ignored.

A homeless man walks into a large, powerful law firm in Washington DC and holds nine attorneys, including the main character, hostage. "You walk right by me as I sit and beg. You spend more on fancy coffee than I do on meals. Why can't you help the poor, the sick, the homeless? You have so much," the man calmly challenges.

One of his demands is to see their tax records, which he checks for their charitable contributions. "Three million dollars," he said in disgust, "and not a dime for the sick and hungry. You are miserable people."

When his captor meets a violent end, Michael is shaken to his core. The experience leaves him a different man. He begins to wonder: *What am I doing to help the poor? What made this stranger leave the streets to attack the corporate world?*

Unable to dismiss the man from his mind, Michael starts down a path he avoided before. His corporate world and self-ambition had blinded him from the world of soup kitchens and free clinics. But the overwhelming needs of those in poverty soon pierce his heart and nurture a growing compassion. He relinquishes his prestige and power to make a difference for others and grows richer emotionally and spiritually.

Often the first step in nurturing compassion is to get out of our daily world and open our eyes to how others live. What is it like not knowing when you will eat again? To live where bullets penetrate your unheated and sparsely furnished apartment? To rock your baby, knowing you have no money for medicine? The barrier of our blind and selfish hearts blocks the flow of God's love into the lives of others.

Danger and injustice opened Michael's eyes to the pain around him. We don't need a life-threatening experience to discover the impact of poverty on the lives of others and how we have ignored their pleas for help. God's words of wisdom direct us toward justice for the poor.

The words of English reformer John Bradford remind us to reach out to others: "There but for the grace of God go I."

The righteous care about justice for the poor,
but the wicked have no such concern.

PROVERBS 29:7 NIV

For Further Thought

1. How do you respond to the poor around you—for instance, the homeless living on the streets?

2. What can you do today to make the life (or lives) of someone less fortunate than yourself better?

I've read this book ❑

My Star Review ☆ ☆ ☆ ☆ ☆

A TALE OF TWO CITIES

Author
CHARLES DICKENS, 1812–1870

First published
SERIALIZED IN *ALL THE YEAR ROUND*
PUBLISHED IN 1859

Original publisher
CHAPMAN & HALL, LONDON

Notes
- HAS SOLD OVER 200 MILLION COPIES
- THE 1935 FILM WAS NOMINATED FOR
  THE BEST PICTURE OSCAR

The Ultimate Demonstration

*C*harles Dickens sweeps us into the world of revolutionary France with the first words of his classic *A Tale of Two Cities*: "It was the best of times, it was the worst of times."

For French émigré Charles Darnay, both were true. He found love and happiness in his new country, England; but disaster persisted in dogging his steps. Early in the story, Darnay was arrested as a French spy. His life hung in the balance until advocate Sydney Carton intervened. Carton was Darnay's doppelgänger, and the prosecution's witness retracted his identification. The jury found in the defendant's favor.

In Darnay, Carton saw everything he could be, wanted to be, and wasn't. They both loved the same woman, Lucie Manette. Carton visited the family from time to time, soaking up Lucie's goodness even as he continued his immoral ways. Years passed, the Bastille fell, and Darnay returned to the land of his birth to rescue a family servant from prison. An aristocrat by birth, although he renounced his title, Darnay was imprisoned and sentenced to death.

Carton coerced a prison guard to allow him into Darnay's cell. He drugged him and took his place at the guillotine. As he faced death, he thought about the promise of the resurrection. His final thoughts revealed his faith: "It is a far, far better thing that I have done than I have done before. It is a far, far better rest that I have gone to."

Dickens might have been thinking of Romans 5:7 when he wrote *A Tale of Two Cities*. The antihero, Sidney Carton, dares to die for the good man, Charles Darnay. As compelling as *A Tale of Two Cities* reads, it is a work of fiction. It only shadows the greatest story of all—the good news of Jesus Christ.

Carton's sacrifice touches and moves us. How much more should the Gospel compel us to action? Imagine if Darnay and Carton exchanged places, and the good man died for the bad. Unthinkable!

Yet that is exactly what God did. When we were sentenced to death for our sin, Christ died in our place. Unlike Darnay, we were *not* good; in fact, we were God's enemies.

The next time we doubt God's love, let us remember the cross.

Very few people will die to save the life of someone else.
Although perhaps for a good person someone might possibly
die. But God shows his great love for us in this way:
Christ died for us while we were still sinners.

ROMANS 5:7–8 NCV

For Further Thought

1. What was your response when someone
    first told you that Christ died for *you*? What
    does His sacrificial death mean to you now?

2. Have you ever come to a point of doubting
    that God loves you? What were the
    circumstances, and what did you do, or
    where did you look, to find assurance of
    His love?

I've read this book ❏

My Star Review ☆ ☆ ☆ ☆ ☆

TO KILL A MOCKINGBIRD

Author

HARPER LEE, BORN 1926

First published

1960

Original publisher

J. B. LIPPINCOTT & CO., PHILADELPHIA

Notes

- WON THE PULITZER PRIZE FOR FICTION IN 1961
- THE AMERICAN FILM INDUSTRY PLACED *MOCKINGBIRD* 25TH IN ITS 100 GREATEST FILMS

THE SACRIFICE

Scout and Jem Finch have what seems like an idyllic childhood. The children in Harper Lee's *To Kill a Mockingbird* lack a mother (as did the author), but they are loved, educated, and left to explore their world—within certain boundaries.

Lee's description of life in Maycomb County doesn't avoid the harsher realities. She explains there are the common folk like the Finch family who obey the law and others whose activities need special allowances. Those others include racists, drunks, and people who lock their children away.

The "others" come out in force when Atticus Finch, a lawyer and the children's father, defends a black man accused of rape. Everyone thinks him innocent, but everyone knows he will be found guilty, because his "victim" was a white woman.

Atticus tries—and fails. The accused man is shot dead in prison.

Despite seeing evil done in front of his eyes, Atticus stays true to his faith. He tells his children it is never right to hate—not even someone like Hitler!

According to folklore, it's a sin to kill a mockingbird because they harm no creature and live only to bring pleasure through their song. Scout and Jem's mockingbird will turn out to be the boy down the street.

Boo Radley was locked away to spare his family social embarrassment. Years later the children try to tease this ghostly presence out into the light, but he never comes. Instead, eventually, he leaves them gifts.

When Bob Ewell, the drunken father of the girl who falsely cried rape, decides to take revenge on Atticus, Boo Radley is finally drawn from his hiding place. Ewell tries to kill Scout. Radley runs to her rescue, killing Ewell.

The local sheriff decides no action should be taken. Boo Radley is never seen again. He spent the first half of his life paying for imagined sins. He spends the second half in hiding after committing the real sin of taking a life—to save Scout. Boo Radley was the town's sacrificial lamb.

In our world, just like in Maycomb County, good is neighbor to evil. It takes real faith to walk amongst it, like Atticus, while refusing to succumb to hate.

Boo Radley saves Scout in a tragically human way: through violence. The rest of us are saved in a more beautiful, more powerful way. Our mockingbird, our sacrificial Lamb, saved us through love.

*He is the atoning sacrifice for our sins, and not only for ours
but also for the sins of the whole world.*

I JOHN 2:2 NIV

For Further Thought

1. How does the self-sacrificial nature of the love of Christ motivate you to treat others and to share your faith with others?

2. What does it mean to you that Jesus Christ is the "atoning sacrifice" for your sins *and* for the sins of the whole world?

I've read this book ❏

My Star Review ☆ ☆ ☆ ☆ ☆

TOM SAWYER

Author

MARK TWAIN, 1835–1910

First published

1876

Original publisher

CHATTO & WINDUS, LONDON

Notes

- TWAIN THOUGHT THIS THE FIRST NOVEL PRODUCED ON A TYPEWRITER
- THE FIRST OF MANY FILM VERSIONS APPEARED IN 1907

UNDER THE CROSS

*M*ark Twain wasn't kidding when he called his book *The* Adventures *of Tom Sawyer.* Tom, Joe Harper, and Huckleberry Finn fill the school holiday with adventures that would make other twelve-year-old boys green with envy. Abandoning all responsibility, they run away from home and become pirates, Robin Hood and his merry men, and treasure hunters. Along the way, Tom finds his first love, Becky.

Tom Sawyer is generally seen as a more "civilized" version of Huckleberry Finn, a boy who sleeps in barrels and eats scraps. He could have been Huckleberry—but he could have been worse. As an orphan in a "one horse town," Tom could easily have become another Injun Joe, an outcast and criminal.

He visits the graveyard with a dead cat in search of a wart remedy; Injun Joe is there, body-snatching. Tom revisits town after faking his death; Injun Joe returns in disguise after being run out of town. Tom goes digging for treasure in the same place Joe buries his ill-gotten silver.

While his moral compass seems to point in no particular direction for any length of time, Tom is repeatedly saved by the love of others. His mother's sister takes him into her home and constantly searches for the best in him. His friends and the townspeople constantly forgive his reckless misadventures.

When Tom Sawyer sees Injun Joe commit a murder, it's time to put up or shut up—so Tom shuts up! Only when an innocent man is nearly hanged does he speak out. Then he and Injun Joe are set on a course that brings them both to a special place.

Deep underground, in a place Injun Joe refers to as "under the cross," both meet their fate. Injun Joe dies, but Tom, concerned with saving Becky, emerges from the ground—born again if you like—to a world where he is a hero, and a rich hero at that.

Still, this is the irrepressible Tom Sawyer—and even with every possible blessing at his feet, he contemplates a future as a robber! How human! How like so many of us! The lure of adventure can be very enticing, especially because it's often the easy way out. A life spent doing the right thing is a much harder path to follow.

That's why we should be glad God gives us what the townsfolk gave Tom Sawyer—innumerable "second" chances!

"I, even I, am he who blots out your transgressions, for my own sake, and remembers your sins no more."

Isaiah 43:25 niv

For Further Thought

1. Can you remember times in your life when you really needed one of God's "second chances"? What were the circumstances?

2. Read Isaiah 43:25 again. Why does God blot out your sins, never to remember them again?

I've read this book ❏

My Star Review ☆ ☆ ☆ ☆ ☆

A TREE GROWS IN BROOKLYN

Author
BETTY SMITH, 1896–1972

First published
1943

Original publisher
HARPER & BROTHERS, NEW YORK

Notes
- ADAPTED INTO A 1951 BROADWAY MUSICAL
- THE 1945 FILM (ELIA KAZAN'S DIRECTORIAL DEBUT) WON TWO ACADEMY AWARDS

PERSEVERING IN ADVERSITY

A Tree Grows in Brooklyn by Betty Smith is the story of first-generation immigrants Katie and Johnny Nolan and their children, Francie and Neeley, and the courage, hope, and hard work that enables them to survive hardship and extreme poverty in Brooklyn, New York, in the early nineteenth century.

The Nolans face hardships such as few work opportunities, scant food, and no money for luxuries like Christmas trees, a second outfit, or coal to stay warm in winter. They don't whine but carry on with steadfast courage, creativity, industry, and stubborn pride. Practical Katie cleans houses for a living, and Johnny, a happy-go-lucky dreamer, is a waiter who, due to his drinking, works only sporadically. When he works, he wears a worn tuxedo and derby hat and often sings for his customers.

The Nolans consider education and the possibility of owning a small plot of land as the keys to freedom and a better life. To become educated, Katie requires her children to listen to, and eventually read on their own, a page from Shakespeare and a page from the Bible each evening before bed. In hopes of owning land, the Nolans skimp when they can and deposit their savings in a tin-can bank. Often, emergencies like medical expenses or work necessities require that they delve into their savings, and it is not until Johnny dies that the almost twenty dollars is used to purchase a small piece of land for his burial.

Although they miss Johnny, whom they all loved dearly, Katie, Francie, and Neeley courageously look for ways to make ends meet. Francie and Neeley pretend to be older than they are and find jobs to help support their mother and raise the baby who arrives a few months after their father's death. Despite having to work diligently, Francie and Neeley manage to attend school and even college.

The story of the Nolans' lives has inspired readers for generations. The book was a nationwide best seller when it came out in 1943, and many copies were sent to servicemen overseas. The Nolans' mettle, which enabled them to stand strong through the trials, is worth emulating and reminds us of the strength of character required to build a life of freedom and opportunity.

*Blessed is the man who perseveres under trial, because when
he has stood the test, he will receive the crown of life
that God has promised to those who love him.*

JAMES 1:12 NIV

For Further Thought

1. How important do you believe
   perseverance is in the Christian life?
   What kinds of things must we believers
   persevere against?

2. What kinds of things most inspire you
   toward perseverance during times of
   difficulty and trial?

I've read this book ❑

My Star Review ☆ ☆ ☆ ☆ ☆

THE VELVETEEN RABBIT

Author

MARGERY WILLIAMS, 1881–1944

First published

1922

Original publisher

AVON BOOKS, NEW YORK

Notes

- WINNER OF THE IRA/CBC CHILDREN'S CHOICE AWARD
- IN THE 1984 *ENCHANTED MUSICAL PLAYHOUSE*, MARIE OSMOND PLAYED THE VELVETEEN RABBIT

BECOMING REAL

*T*he world is full of people, but how many of them are real? Many are so wrapped up in what they can get that they never spare a thought for what they can give—or where they might be going!

The nursery in Margery Williams's *The Velveteen Rabbit* is full of toys like that. Mechanical toys proud of their workings, porcelain toys in love with their shiny surfaces, even toys with government connections! But one of them is real. And one wants to be.

The Skin Horse tells the Velveteen Rabbit that becoming real is something that happens when you are loved. "Does it hurt?" the Velveteen Rabbit asks. It does, the Skin Horse admits, but you don't mind when you are real.

Becoming real, whether you are a rabbit or a human, means stepping out from the crowd and setting yourself up as a target for all those who don't know what love is or what it does. It can hurt, but it's worth it.

The boy who owns all the toys loves the Velveteen Rabbit, and in return the rabbit sees him through a bout of scarlet fever. Then the doctor orders all the boy's clothes and toys to be burned. The Velveteen Rabbit finds himself in a sack, waiting to be thrown on the bonfire.

The Velveteen Rabbit cries a *real* tear. He has loved and been loved. The Skin Horse was right. It did hurt. Does he regret it? Do those who have lived in Christ's love regret the rocky path they often walk?

The Velveteen Rabbit's tear brings the Nursery Magic Fairy. Like the Holy Spirit will do for a beaten, scared human, the Nursery Magic Fairy transforms the threadbare Velveteen Rabbit. She makes him more than he ever thought he could be and all he ever wished to be. More than that, she takes him to where there are many others just like him. He's not velveteen anymore, but real and free.

Becoming real is a journey for many Christians, but it's a journey begun. It begins with His love, which is already there, and it ends when we completely accept it and love Him back.

There might be hurt and heartache along the way, but what would you rather do? Be like the others, the unreal ones, and wait until your porcelain cracks? Or until your mainspring pops?

*May the grace of the Lord Jesus Christ, and the love of God,
and the fellowship of the Holy Spirit be with you all.*

2 CORINTHIANS 13:14 NIV

For Further Thought

1. Can you think of a time when walking in
    Christ's love took you on a rocky path?
    What benefits did you receive from
    continuing the journey?

2. What do you do with the hurt and
    heartache you experience in your walk
    with Jesus? What do you believe God
    wants you to do with it?

I've read this book ❏

My Star Review ☆ ☆ ☆ ☆ ☆

WAR OF THE WORLDS

Author
H. G. Wells, 1866–1946

First published
Serialized by *Pearson's Magazine*, 1897
Published in 1898

Original publisher
William Heinemann, London

Notes
- Has been continuously in print since 1898
- The 2005 Stephen Speilberg film starred Tom Cruise

AT THE DAWN OF LIFE

*I*t's said that H. G. Wells wrote *The War of the Worlds* as a protest against the evils of Empire. Perhaps, but the evil he embodies in the Martians comes from "the Pit," and it affects the whole world.

"The Pit" Wells repeatedly refers to is the crater left by the Martians' spacecraft. When they first emerge, they seem weak, ungainly, of no real threat. And so it is with little evils, broken promises, and petty thefts. We think nothing of them.

Wells's narrator considers several ways in which the aliens might easily be defeated.

The onlookers give the Martians time, even selling sweets at the side of the Pit—and the Martians use that delay to build their fighting machines. While ordinary people look on, thinking of ways to profit from what has happened, evil grows and becomes unstoppable.

Wells makes the point that the fighting machines may be extraterrestrial but evil isn't. "What are these

Martians?" a desperate person asks. "What are we?" the narrator replies.

But perhaps evil isn't all bad. There must be a purpose, or why would God allow it? The purpose becomes clear when, in hundreds of little ways, people rise above petty self-interest to help others. The sailors on the ironclad *Thunder Child* put themselves between three Martian fighting machines and a ship full of civilians, knowing they must die but still determined to buy others a little more life.

It's in extreme times, when we face fear and evil, that we have the chance to be what God knows we can be. Those are the times we aspire to be most Christlike, when we are willing to give everything away for love.

Despite great heroism and noble sacrifice, the Martian machines seem set to ravage the earth. Then, for no obvious reason, the aliens begin to die.

Wells's narrator realizes the aliens have been laid low by "the humblest things that God, in his wisdom, has put on this earth"—bacteria! The narrator kneels, extends his hands to the sky, and begins thanking God.

As a man of faith, perhaps he should not have been surprised that even when he was being tried to the fullest extent, even when his world seemed to be falling apart, plans drawn up at the very dawn of life were, invisibly, in motion. Evil would not win.

He was already saved!

*They marched across the breadth of the earth and surrounded
the camp of God's people, the city he loves. But fire came
down from heaven and devoured them.*

REVELATION 20:9 NIV

For Further Thought

1. How do you respond to those who question how or why a God who identifies Himself as being so good allows such evil to take place in the world?

2. What do you believe will happen to all evil when Christ returns?

I've read this book ❏

My Star Review ☆ ☆ ☆ ☆ ☆

THE WATER BABIES

Author

CHARLES KINGSLEY, 1819–1875

First published

SERIALIZED IN 1862–63 FOR *MACMILLAN'S MAGAZINE*, PUBLISHED IN 1863

Original publisher

MACMILLAN & CO., LONDON & CAMBRIDGE

Notes

- EXTREMELY POPULAR IN ITS TIME BUT REGARDED AS POLITICALLY INCORRECT TODAY
- FILMED AS A MIX OF ANIMATION AND LIVE-ACTION IN 1978

"I Will Be a Fish"

*T*hose that wish to be clean, clean they will be; and those that wish to be foul, foul they will be." The sentiment sums up the spirit—if not the style—of Charles Kingsley's 1863 novel *The Water Babies*. Kingsley is strong on redemption, and this book is a beautiful example of the triumph of hope over experience.

Tom, the unlikely hero, is dirty, rude, and not averse to throwing stones at passing gentry. His life is spent half in tears, half in laughter, with very little by way of thought in between. He is a near-feral child, made to sweep chimneys by a master who pays him in blows.

After getting lost in the chimneys of a mansion, Tom steps from a fireplace into Ellie's world. Ellie is clean, beautiful, and good. To Tom, she seems like "an angel out of heaven."

Seeing Ellie, Tom realizes he is dirty and cries in shame.

The adults of the house take him for a burglar and

chase him across the moor. He runs to the river, declaring, "I will be a fish; I will swim in the water; I must be clean, I must be clean!"

Tom dies in the river, but he finds new life and a series of Wonderland-like adventures as a water baby. He meets Mr. Doasyouwouldbedoneby and Mrs. Bedonebyasyoudid, and he tries to avoid the Examiner-of-all-Examiners.

Along the way, Tom learns to do things for reasons other than self-interest and to help those he would rather not—which brings him, eventually, to Mr. Grimes, his former master. Mrs. Bedonebyasyoudid has Grimes trapped in a chimney where no one can help him but himself. Grimes is one of those who "wish to be foul"—until Tom tells a story of Grimes's mother. The sullen master sweep cries tears of real repentance that sweep away the very mortar between the bricks of his prison.

In the end, Tom is reborn as a man and reunited with Ellie because he had "done the things he did not like."

The things we do not like to do are often the things that ask the most of us—like loving our enemies. The effort required is huge, but the reward is a cleansing of the soul—rebirth into a purer form. Christ is a fisher of men, and in the end, through trial and forgiveness, Tom becomes a fish worth catching!

"And now what are you waiting for? Get up, be baptized and wash your sins away, calling on his name."

ACTS 22:16 NIV

For Further Thought

1. Think of something God calls you to do but that you would rather not do. How do you approach obedience to God in doing that very thing?

2. In what ways do you strive to follow Jesus' invitation to be a "fisher of men"?

I've read this book ❏

My Star Review ☆ ☆ ☆ ☆ ☆

WHITE FANG

Author
Jack London, 1876–1916

First published
1906

Original publisher
Macmillan Publishers, USA

Notes
- A companion volume to London's
  Call of the Wild
- Filmed by Disney in 1991 with a sequel in 1994

BLESSED WOLF

$\mathcal{J}$ack London's *White Fang* begins with chilling description of "The Wild." It is savage, frozen-hearted, and with a laugh as cold as frost. The Wild sees life as an offense. It is the main theme of the book, and it has two creatures. One is White Fang, a wolf, and the other is Jim Hall, the human equivalent of a wolf.

White Fang's fight begins at birth. Desperate times leave him the only survivor of his litter. A tribe of Native Americans takes White Fang in, but the other dogs fear him from the outset. They recognize The Wild in him and exclude him. In return, he becomes "the enemy of his kind" just to survive.

White Fang is soon traded for a bottle of whiskey. His new owner puts the wolf's instincts to good use in dogfights. White Fang is the deadliest fighter around until he momentarily leaves his throat exposed. A bulldog takes the chance, and White Fang is on the verge of death, when Weedon Scott buys his life.

Scott and White Fang don't always hit it off. The wolf has his instincts to overcome and the man has prejudice to battle. Despite the mockery of others, Scott treats his new "dog" with endless patience and kindness. White Fang comes to see him as "the love-master." Love, eventually, inspires devotion.

Jim Hall has much in common with White Fang: "He had not been born right and he had not been helped any by the molding he received at the hands of society."

Undoubtedly guilty, but not of the crime he is arrested for, Hall is sentenced to life by an unwitting Judge Scott, Weedon Scott's father. He escapes and comes seeking revenge.

White Fang is waiting. The two creatures of The Wild come together in a deadly struggle. Both are hard, strong, and ruthless, but they are no longer the same. Both have been lost, but one has found redemption. One is fighting for hatred, the other for love.

After his recovery, White Fang's adoptive family refers to him as "Blessed Wolf." It's a term that perfectly describes the options we face. Weedon Scott paid for White Fang, but White Fang had to choose to accept his love. Jesus paid for each of us, so the blessing is ours to take. So, do we choose The Wild, or do we choose Love?

Remember, Love wins!

"In the same way, I tell you, there is rejoicing in the presence of the angels of God over one sinner who repents."

LUKE 15:10 NIV

For Further Thought

1. What factors do you think keep some people from choosing the way of Christ's love but instead lead them to choose "the Wild"?

2. What can you do today to demonstrate the love of Jesus Christ to someone close to you?

I've read this book ❑

My Star Review ☆ ☆ ☆ ☆ ☆

WINNIE THE POOH

Author
A. A. MILNE, 1882–1956

First published
1926

Original publisher
METHUEN & CO., LONDON

Notes
- A LATIN TRANSLATION, *WINNIE ILLE PU*, REACHED THE *NEW YORK TIMES* BEST SELLER LIST
- BECAME ONE OF DISNEY'S MOST SUCCESSFUL FRANCHISES

STUCK WITH POOH BEAR

A favorite story from A. A. Milne's *Winnie the Pooh* is "Pooh Goes Visiting and Gets into a Tight Place." On a visit to Rabbit's home, Pooh overstuffs himself with honey. He then tries to climb out the door but—"Oh, help!"—poor Pooh is stuck.

Rabbit tries to pull Pooh out, but he won't budge. Pooh blames Rabbit for not having a big enough front door, but Rabbit says sternly, "It all comes of eating too much." So Rabbit fetches Christopher Robin, who sees what's happened and smiles lovingly. "Silly old Bear," he says, in such a way that Pooh feels hopeful again.

Pooh must wait until he gets thin again. Christopher Robin reads "a Sustaining Book, such as would help and comfort a Wedged Bear in Great Tightness." At week's end, Christopher Robin says, "Now!" and he, Rabbit, and Rabbit's friends and relations yank Pooh's paws.

Pooh says, "Oh!" and "Ow!" until *pop!*—he's free.

With a nod of thanks, he continues on his way,

humming proudly to himself.

Reading this story, we, along with Christopher Robin, smile and say, "Silly old Bear!" But there's a lesson to learn from Pooh—a lesson about sin. Pooh Bear has a problem with gluttony—he overeats to the point that he gets stuck in a hole. Then he tries to cast blame on others—namely Rabbit and his front door. But Christopher Robin loves him enough to offer hope and wise counsel and even reads him a "Sustaining Book" while he waits for the consequences of his gluttony to pass. And then Pooh's friends care enough to yank him out.

We, too, have pet sins. For some it's gluttony, for others it's lying, lust, stealing, anger. . .the list goes on and on. No matter the sin, we get stuck in it. Without Christ loving us enough to come and offer hope and help, we'd never get free. And God has even given us a "Sustaining Book"—the Bible—to help us along the way and friends to pull us out of trouble.

Once we get free, though, we mustn't forget, like Pooh does in Disney's version of this story. He pops from the hole and goes straight into a bee tree, where he gluts on honey once again, totally forgetting the freedom he just won. If we don't remember what we're saved from, we, too, will go right back into bondage to our pet sin.

Therefore, since we have so great a cloud of witnesses surrounding us, let us also lay aside every encumbrance and the sin which so easily entangles us, and let us run with endurance the race that is set before us.

HEBREWS 12:1 NASB

For Further Thought

1. Can you think of one or more "small" sins that keep you stuck where you are? What keeps you from claiming the freedom Christ has brought to those who trust in and walk with Him?

2. God promises to forgive and forget our sins when we confess them to Him. But how helpful do you think remembering where you came from is in keeping you from ending up there again?

I've read this book ❑

My Star Review ☆ ☆ ☆ ☆ ☆

A WRINKLE IN TIME

Author
MADELEINE L'ENGLE, 1918–2007

First published
1962

Original publisher
FARRAR, STRAUS & GIROUX, NEW YORK

Notes
- WON THE NEWBERRY MEDAL AND SEQUOYAH BOOK AWARD
- FILMED FOR TV BY DISNEY IN 2003

CELEBRATING EQUALITY. . .
AND VARIETY

*M*adeleine L'Engle's Newbery Medal-winning fantasy *A Wrinkle in Time* tells of three children's time-traveling adventures. Meg and Charles Wallace Murry, along with their friend Calvin O'Keefe, meet Mrs. Who, Mrs. Which, and Mrs. Whatsit and find out that they must "tesser," or wrinkle in time, to rescue Meg and Charles Wallace's father from Camazotz. A dark planet, Camazotz is where the people have given up the battle against evil. IT, the bodiless being that dominates Camazotz, controls their minds and imprisons Mr. Murry because he won't give up his will. IT wants to dominate the children as well.

IT gains control over Charles Wallace and uses him to try to persuade Meg to align herself with IT. Playing on Meg's unhappiness at not fitting in with other kids, IT argues that everyone on Camazotz is happy because they are all the same and therefore equal. But Meg comes to a realization that saves her: "Like and equal are two entirely different things."

Meg understands that equality does not mean people act or think or live completely alike. She realizes it's okay that Charles Wallace is a five-year-old genius who rarely speaks outside his family, and that basketball star Calvin comes from a horrible family but is great with words. She learns it's all right that she's great at math but gawky and uncomfortable with people. And ultimately, foolish, weak Meg uses her stubborn love to help her rescue her father and brother from IT's clutches.

As Christians, we must also remember that *like* and *equal* are not the same. While God is the head of the Church and we act within the parameters He's set for us, we have freedom to be ourselves. Mrs. Whatsit compares our lives to a sonnet—a very strict form of poetry that allows the poet freedom to say what he or she pleases within that form. God created us with equal value and gave us the same set of rules to live by. But He also gave each person his or her own personality, looks, talents, likes, and dislikes.

So, instead of condemning a fellow Christian for his or her differences, we should celebrate the variety God created for His own glory. We should rejoice in the magnificent jumble that makes up Christ's kingdom.

*Now there are varieties of gifts, but the same Spirit.
And there are varieties of ministries, and the same Lord.
There are varieties of effects, but the same God who
works all things in all persons.*

1 CORINTHIANS 12:4–6 NASB

For Further Thought

1. How do you usually respond to a fellow
   believer who thinks differently from you or
   who likes things you don't like and doesn't
   like things you do?

2. What can you do today to begin
   tolerating—even celebrating—the
   differences between yourself and other
   believers?

I've read this book ❑

My Star Review ☆ ☆ ☆ ☆ ☆

WUTHERING HEIGHTS

Author
EMILY BRONTË, 1818–1848

First published
1847

Original publisher
THOMAS CAUTLEY NEWBY, LONDON

Notes
- THE ONLY NOVEL PUBLISHED BY EMILY BRONTË
- THE 1939 FILM HAS BEEN PRESERVED BY THE US NATIONAL FILM REGISTRY

WASTED LAND, WASTED LOVE

*T*he stormy and passionate relationship between Heathcliff and Catherine serves as the foundation of Emily Brontë's classic *Wuthering Heights*. The frequent storms and wind sweeping through the isolated moors of the English countryside symbolize the turbulence these characters create in their acts of revenge and deception. Love only begins to grow in the next generation as age-old vengeance fades away.

The ancient manor of Wuthering Heights provides the backdrop to a story told by a housekeeper to a traveler renting a neighboring home. Catherine's father brings Heathcliff to Wuthering Heights as a foster child. Catherine's brother, Hindley, is full of jealously and treats Heathcliff with cruelty and revenge. But Catherine quickly learns to love him, and the two become inseparable, spending many days together on the moors.

The moors where Catherine and Heathcliff play are soggy, wind-whipped, and infertile wasteland that cannot be cultivated. Navigation is very difficult and dangerous due to the uneven terrain and the frequent unexpected storms.

Heathcliff leaves after Hindley treats him as a common laborer. Bent on vengeance, he returns years later, shortly after Catherine marries a neighbor.

As Heathcliff seeks revenge on those who hurt him, he loans money to a now-alcoholic Hindley and eventually inherits Wuthering Heights.

Catherine dies in childbirth and her daughter, named after her mother, grows up to marry Heathcliff's frail and sickly son. This marriage is all part of Heathcliff's vengeful plan to obtain and control all the land and the lives he touches.

After Heathcliff's and his son's deaths, the younger Catherine finally finds love and happiness with her cousin, Hareton. Catherine, who at first made fun of Hareton, slowly sees him with new eyes and patiently finds the love all of the other characters desperately sought.

The characters in *Wuthering Heights* illustrate our deep desire to be loved and how easily our frail egos can be broken. Anger and revenge accomplish little and often lead us on the road away from love.

Love blooms best in the rich soil of God's patience, our humility, and a gentle attitude of accepting people as they are. The stunted plants on the moor reflect the inability of anything to flourish or grow normally at Wuthering Heights, just as the characters find it difficult to fulfill their own strong passions and seek aid from outside sources to realize their deepest needs.

Both land and people need the right kind of soil and nourishment to grow and survive.

Be completely humble and gentle;
be patient, bearing with one another in love.

Ephesians 4:2 niv

For Further Thought

1. What kinds of things do you find yourself intolerant of in other believers? Ask yourself if those things are valid, or if they are your own personal biases.

2. Do you consider yourself a patient person? What kinds of things make you impatient, and what can you do to make yourself more patient about those things?

I've read this book ❑

My Star Review ☆ ☆ ☆ ☆ ☆

SCRIPTURE INDEX